BEAUTIFUL THINGS TO MAKE FOR
BRIDES

CONTENTS

EDITORIAL
Craft Editor: Tonia Todman
Food Editor: Sheryle Eastwood
Managing Editor: Judy Poulos
Editor: Marian Broderick
Editorial Co-ordinator: Margaret Kelly
Text: Mary Jane Bailey
Assistant Craft Editor: Sally Pereira
Assistant Food Editor: Rachel Blackmore
Sewing and craft assistance: Martina Oprey,
Yvonne Deacon, Louise Pfanner, Gill Fury, Kate
Fury, Suzanne Lynch

DESIGN AND PRODUCTION
Sheridan Carter
Kirsten Tona
Chris Hatcher
Barbara Martusewicz

ILLUSTRATIONS
Kim Bywater

PHOTOGRAPHY
Andrew Elton
Food Styling: Carolyn Fienberg

PUBLISHER
Philippa Sandall

Family Circle is a registered trademark of IPC
Magazines Ltd.
Published by J. B. Fairfax Press Ltd by
arrangement with IPC Magazines Ltd

(c) J. B. Fairfax Press Pty Ltd, 1990
This book is copyright. Apart from any fair dealing
for the purpose of private study, research, criticism
or review, as permitted under the Copyright Act, no
part may be reproduced by any process without the
written permission of the publisher. Enquiries
should be made in writing to the publisher.

Beautiful Things to Make for Brides
Includes Index
ISBN 1 86343 006 7

Formatted by J.B. Fairfax Press Pty Ltd
Output by Adtype, Sydney
Printed by Toppan Printing Co, Hong Kong
Distributed by J.B. Fairfax Press Ltd
9 Trinity Centre, Park Farm Estate
Wellingborough, Northants
Ph: (0933) 402330 Fax: (0933) 402234

COVER
Photography by John Waddy
Graphic Design by Frank Pithers
Styling by Sally Hirst
Hair and Make-up by Lesley Cameron
Dresses by Sylvia Chan
Flowers by Carla Florist
Jewellery by Christopher Essex
Backdrop Fabric by Home Yardage

MEASURING UP

Metric	Inches	Cups	
2 mm	$1/16$	¼ cup	60 mL
6 mm	¼	⅓ cup	80 mL
1 cm	$3/8$	½ cup	125 mL
2.5 cm	1	1 cup	250 mL
5 cm	2		
30 cm	12	**Spoons**	
91 cm	36	¼ teaspoon	1.25 mL
		½ teaspoon	2.5 mL
		1 teaspoon	5 mL
		1 tablespoon	20 mL

For measuring ingredients in our recipes we have used a nest of metric measuring cups and a set of metric measuring spoons. All cup and spoon measures are level.

QUICK METRIC IMPERIAL CONVERTER

g	oz	mL	fl.oz
30	1	30	1
60	2	60	2
125	4	125	4
250	8	250	8
370	12	370	12
500	16	500	16

BRIDE TO BE

A wedding is a very special event for the bride-to-be, her family and good friends. This book is full of wonderful ideas for making the occasion even more special by adding the very personal touch that comes from the work of loving hands. It's not the spectacular but the small details, often handmade, which give a wedding its atmosphere and style.

Add a touch of individuality to all the time-honoured traditions – the invitations to be sent out, orders of service to be followed, and thank you notes.

To ensure your wedding goes without a hitch, follow our guidelines for wedding etiquette, for calculating your wedding and honeymoon budgets and for selecting the perfect dress to ensure you truly are queen of the day! There are also imaginative suggestions for setting up your home, treats that friends and family can make to fill your pantry shelves, or frilled and embroidered luxuries for a romantic trousseau. Use our ideas as inspiration for devising plans, and making gowns, bouquets and wedding cakes with a confident and imaginative hand. Make your wedding a special day for everyone to treasure always.

HERE COMES THE
BRIDE

*Getting married can be quite a complicated business. Use
this simple guide to steer you smoothly step by step through
the necessary arrangements and legal requirements.
Our Bridal Calendar and Budget will provide you with
helpful pointers for your wedding plans.*

Whether you plan to marry in a church, a garden or in a registry office, or even if it is your second marriage, there are laws by which you have to abide. The marriage must be solemnised by a minister of religion, a registrar or an authorised celebrant and generally some notice of your intention to marry must be registered. If either one of you has been married previously, certificates showing that you are free to marry, such as a copy of a decree absolute or death certificate must be presented. You must also produce a birth certificate, or perhaps a passport, to verify your age. In spite of obvious changes in lifestyle, traditional Church weddings are still popular amongst today's brides.

For the **Anglican** and **Church of England** ceremony, the groom and best man should be the first people to enter the church. They should arrive about 15 minutes before the service is to begin and wait in the vestry. Ushers direct the guests to their pews, with the groom's parents, relatives and friends to the right side of the church and the bride's family and friends to the left. The processional music begins when the bride and her father reach

Photography by Alan Khan and Christopher Poulos

With this ring
I thee wed ...

the entrance of the church. All the guests rise, and the bridegroom and his attendants take their places at the chancel steps with the groom nearest to the aisle. Traditionally, the bride leads the procession on her father's arm unless there is a flowergirl, and the bridesmaids follow to help with her veil and train. However, in recent years many brides prefer the custom of following the bridesmaids into the church.

The Anglican service usually takes about 30 minutes, after which the minister leads the bride and groom and attendants into the vestry to sign the church register and certificates of marriage. Once these formalities are completed, the bridal party proceeds down the aisle with the bride and groom in the lead.

There are two types of services in the **Roman Catholic** church: a Nuptial Mass which includes the celebration of the Eucharist or a wedding ceremony only. The latter is usually chosen when one of the parties is not Catholic. A formal wedding usually takes place in the afternoon, although some Catholic weddings follow morning Mass. Contact your local priest at least two to three months before you plan to marry in order to receive instructions and complete the necessary paperwork. If you are not marrying at your local parish you must receive a 'letter of freedom' from your own priest. Banns are published three times (usually on consecutive Sundays) before the wedding in the parish newsletter.

An Italian Catholic ceremony, is generally quite large and can be held at any time of the year except during Holy Week, the week before Easter. Invitations are sent out six weeks before-hand and often have poetry inscribed on the front. Great emphasis is given to photo-graphy as many invited guests may be unable to attend the wedding if they live abroad. Photographs will be sent to all absent friends and family, as a memento. The Italian wedding cake is called 'pan di spagna', a light sponge cake filled with whipped cream and liqueurs. It is customary for the bride to hand out bombonieres to each guest. These are bags of sugared almonds in containers of crystal and tulle.

Most **Greek Orthodox** weddings take place in January or at Easter. They cannot be held during the two weeks before Christmas or during the six weeks of Lent. During the ceremony, garlands of orange blossom, joined by a ribbon, are placed on the heads of the bride and groom. At the reception, it is customary for guests to pin money to the bridal couple's clothing to boost their finances and indicate wishes for their prosperity.

For an **Orthodox Jewish** wedding in a synagogue, the bride and groom must both be Jewish. In mixed marriages, either the non-Jewish member converts to Judaism or the wedding takes place in a registry office. Both parties must apply to the chief rabbi for authorisation to marry at least three weeks before the ceremony. When applying, the bride and groom should be accompanied by at least one witness. A Jewish wedding usually takes place in a synagogue, but it can also be held outdoors as long as it is under a chuppah (canopy).

Weddings cannot be held on the Sabbath or during certain fes-tivals. As in most marriages, the ring is an essential symbol. At the synagogue, the bride enters on her father's arm and is followed by her bridesmaids, the groom's parents, and the bride's mother on the arm of a male relative. During the ceremony the bride stands under a canopy to the right of the groom. The parents stand on either side of the bridal couple.

Photography by Alan Khan and Christopher Poulos

A wedding is a special occasion for the family and friends

Quakers (members of the Religious Society of Friends) also have their own distinctive style of wedding service which dates back to the seventeenth century. A couple announces their inten-tion to marry at the local Sunday meeting and the registering office of the monthly meeting then gives them the necessary forms and information. Marriages can take place at any meeting. They take the same form as a normal meeting for worship, without any

pomp or ceremony. Rings play no formal part in the wedding service, although couples may exchange rings after the vows are taken.

Civil ceremonies in registry offices or elsewhere are usually short and simple. The bridal party should arrive about 10 minutes early so the order of service can be explained and the fees can be paid. The celebrant gives a short address and then the vows are taken. The register is signed by the wedding couple and their witnesses. Rings are not necessarily exchanged.

If you choose to have a civil ceremony you may like to have the marriage blessed in a church afterwards. Usually, this is a simple service with the minister giving a brief address, followed by prayers. Civil ceremonies are less formal than church weddings. Choose a marriage celebrant recommended by friends or relatives. Couples should visit the celebrant before the wedding to discuss the style of ceremony and to complete the necessary forms. Most civil ceremonies do not include hymns and prayers. To personalise the occasion, you can write a poem or text for the celebrant to read aloud or choose a favourite piece of music to be played.

A second marriage can have all the traditional trimmings and formality of a first wedding, especially if it is to be a religious ceremony. There are no set rules about dress for second-time brides so choose whatever suits you and the occasion. The groom should dress to match the formal-ity of the bride's attire. It is acceptable to have young attend-ants, such as daughters and sons, but it is customary for the bride to have only a maid of honour.

B R I D A L
C A L E N D A R

Careful planning is the key to a happy and successful wedding day. If you decide on a formal wedding, begin preparations at least six months in advance (this can be halved for an informal wedding). Remember, although every wedding is different – it may be formal or informal, in a church, a registry office or in your back garden – it's important to plan your wedding so that everything runs smoothly, with a minimum of fuss.

FIRST DECISIONS

❖ Decide on the size and style of the wedding. Once the date is set, arrange a clergyman or celebrant to officiate on the day.

❖ Work out your budget.

❖ Compile a guest list in consultation with both families.

❖ Select and book a reception venue/caterers/band/string quartet.

❖ Choose your attendants: best man, bridesmaids, groomsmen, flower girls, page boys and ushers.

❖ Consider styles for both the bridal gown and bridesmaids' outfits. If you are making them yourself or if you are having them made, patterns, fabrics, sewing and fittings need to be organised.

❖ Decide on a colour theme for the wedding.

❖ Plan the menswear and arrange for necessary hiring.

❖ Think about your trousseau and going-away outfit.

❖ Select a honeymoon destination and make reservations.

❖ Select styles for flowers, stationery, transport, photography, music and catering.

3 MONTHS TO GO

❖ Begin regular visits to a beauty therapist.

❖ Order invitations and other stationery.

❖ Choose weddings rings.

❖ Arrange hire of marquee, cutlery and china if necessary.

❖ Arrange to have your wedding cake made and decorated (it is considered bad luck to make your own).

❖ Arrange for a professional or

Photographs are a lasting reminder of the wedding day

friend to be the official photographer for the day. You may also want a videotape for live footage.

❖ Confirm arrangements with the clergyman, celebrant or registrar, and discuss the form of service you will have, church fees and music.

❖ Discuss bouquets, headdresses and flower arrangements with your florist.

❖ Organise menus for the wedding reception.

❖ Book a local hotel for the night if you are not leaving on your honeymoon until the following day.

❖ Finalise honeymoon plans, passports and visas. Remember, if you plan to change your name, allow plenty of time for new documents, such as passports and cheque books, to be issued.

❖ Plan decorations for pew ends, reception tables and so on.

❖ Plan and organise gifts for bridal party.

2 MONTHS TO GO

❖ Post wedding invitations. Record acceptances as your parents receive them.

❖ Make a list of all wedding gifts received and send thank you letters immediately.

❖ Make arrangements for accommodation of visiting wedding guests.

❖ Plan and order the flowers, or, if you prefer, make dried flower or silk bouquets.

❖ Organise wedding ceremony rehearsals with the minister, celebrant and bridal party.

❖ Arrange with hairstylist, manicurist, beautician for an appointment on the day or day before the wedding. It's a good idea to have a practice make up and hairstyle with your headdress on.

❖ Apply for a marriage licence.

1 MONTH TO GO

❖ Chase up late replies to invitations and finalise guest list.

❖ Write place cards for the reception. Organise cake boxes for guests who cannot attend.

❖ Finalise the menus and wine lists; arrange seating plan for the reception.

❖ Check that all bridal clothes, whether being made or hired, will be ready.

❖ Check that your trousseau is complete.

❖ Prepare a newspaper announcement; most newspapers have ready-printed forms for you to fill in.

❖ It is also a good idea to insure wedding gifts, and to have someone booked to look after gifts received on the day.

❖ Give a bridesmaid's lunch or dinner.

1 WEEK TO GO

❖ Pack for honeymoon.

❖ Hold final rehearsal for the ceremony; check the service sheets.

❖ Wear in your wedding shoes at home.

❖ Arrange the bachelor night for at least one week before the wedding. The bride's night out with her girlfriends could be held the same evening.

ON THE DAY

❖ Attend to all your beauty preparations, then relax and enjoy yourself.

AFTERWARDS

❖ It's easy to forget that things also need to be arranged for after the event – like someone to collect your gown and the groom's suit when you have changed into your going-away outfits.

❖ Wedding presents should be packed away and taken to your home if they were displayed at the reception.

❖ Items borrowed or hired need to be returned promptly.

❖ Post any thank you notes that were written at the last minute.

❖ ACKNOWLEDGEMENTS ❖
If you are too busy to write thank you notes beforehand, send acknowledgement cards on receipt of presents, then follow up with a personal note after the wedding.

BRIDAL BUDGET

A sumptuous wedding need not be too expensive

A wedding is a celebration of love and is a touching and exciting event whether it is simple or lavish. Don't be fooled into over-committing yourselves financially. With flair and imagination costs can be kept to a minimum without losing any of the fun and meaning of the occasion. Organising a wedding can place great strain on available resources, but customs are changing and the costs need no longer be met by the bride's parents alone. Early discussions about who should pay what expenses will help you decide how much to spend in which areas. The most important ingredients are free: planning, consideration and imagination. Once you know your budget, work out your priorities and how

much to spend on flowers, bridal outfits, transport, reception, and honeymoon. Reserve at least 20 per cent of the total budget to cover unforeseen expenses.

WHO PAYS FOR WHAT?

Traditionally, attendants pay for their own transport expenses, attire and the bridal shower and bachelor party. The groom and his family pay for the bride's engagement and wedding rings, celebrant or church fees, gifts for the groom's attendants, flowers for the bridal party, the bride's wedding gift, accommodation for the groom's attendants if necessary and the honeymoon. The bride and her family pay for the invitations and announcements, engagement party, flowers for the ceremony and reception, groom's wedding gift and wedding ring, gifts for the bride's attendants, bridal outfit, accessories and trousseau, all ceremony fees except the celebrant, all photography, accommodation for bridesmaids, transportation for the wedding party and reception expenses. Refer to reference table opposite.

Drawing up a guest list calls for good sense and tact. Both families should write a list of names of friends and family they would like to invite. If the number of guests gets too out-of-hand for the church or for the budget, a tactful way to include everyone is to have a large informal engagement party and keep the wedding small.

The style of wedding will certainly affect the costs. Most formal weddings are held in a church, with abundant flowers and decorations and there may be a soloist or choir as well as the traditional organist.

A semi-formal wedding can be held at almost any time of the

day with any number of people present. The bridal party is often smaller than for a more formal occasion. A bridesmaid or matron of honour and best man may be the only attendants. A general rule for receptions is that the more formal the occasion, the more expensive it is. If you have an early morning wedding, a breakfast/brunch can be served either at home or in the garden; for a mid-morning wedding, the only essentials are cake and champagne; for a noon wedding, a light lunch is usually served and an early to mid-afternoon ceremony could be followed by a high tea. Late-afternoon ceremonies, however, are usually followed by a cocktail party and dinner, either seated or buffet-style, and dancing.

Couples have been upset to find they have forgotten to budget for their honeymoon, so include this in your initial wedding budget. It can be the vacation of your dreams if you take the time to plan carefully. Decide on your destination, the type of accommodation which appeals to you, whether you plan to eat out or have a self-contained apartment where you can cook some meals for yourselves, and how you want to travel – don't forget airport taxes! Other expenses to bear in mind are drinks, entertainment, tips, gifts, mementos and impulse spending, plus spare cash for emergencies.

Our honeymoon checklist below will help you to make all those important decisions.

HONEYMOON CHECKLIST
Decide on:
- [ ] destination
- [ ] type of travel
- [ ] type of accommodation: hotel/motel or self-contained apartment
- [ ] drinks
- [ ] entertainment
- [ ] trips
- [ ] gifts
- [ ] mementos
- [ ] impulse spending
- [ ] spare cash for emergencies

WHO PAYS FOR WHAT?

BRIDE AND FAMILY	BRIDEGROOM AND FAMILY	ATTENDANTS
invitations		bridal shower
engagement party		bachelor party
flowers for ceremony and reception	flowers for bridal party	shower tea
groom's wedding gift and wedding ring	bride's wedding gift and wedding ring	kitchen tea
gifts for bride's attendants	gifts for groom's attendants	wedding present
bridal outfit, accessories and trousseau	own outfit	own outfit
ceremony fees (except for celebrant)	celebrant or church fees	
photography		
accommodation for bridesmaids (if necessary)	accommodation for groom's attendants (if necessary)	
transportation for wedding party		
reception expenses	honeymoon	

CHAMPAGNE
BREAKFAST

Your life together gets off to a delicious start with this special breakfast. Tangy Tomato Cooler, Berry Cornucopia and Grapefruit Compote add colour to the happy occasion.

Back, from left: Strawberry Punch, Tangy Tomato Cooler, Fresh Berry Cornucopia, Grapefruit Compote Cups; centre, from left: Marmalade Muffins, Dill Pikelets with Oysters and Caviar, Potato and Salami Fritatta, Tomato and Spinach Roulade; front, from left: Cheese Pastry Cups with Salmon Souffle, Plain Pancake Stack with mascarpone cheese and honey, Spinach Pancake Stack with smoked salmon and avocado.

GRAPEFRUIT COMPOTE CUPS

As a timesaver, prepare these the day before and store in the refrigerator. Take them out two hours before serving and allow them to return to room temperature.

Serves 10

- [ ] **5 grapefruit**
- [ ] **250 g pitted prunes**
- [ ] **250 g dried apricots**
- [ ] **125 g raisins**
- [ ] **125 g dried peaches**
- [ ] **125 g dried apples**
- [ ] **1/2 cup (125 mL) sweet sherry**
- [ ] **1 cup (250 mL) water**
- [ ] **1 3/4 cups (440 mL) orange juice**
- [ ] **2 tablespoons honey**
- [ ] **2 teaspoons chopped preserved ginger**

1   Cut grapefruit in half crossways. Scoop out pulp without damaging skin and reserve cups. Cut pulp into segments and set aside.

2   Place prunes, apricots, raisins, peaches and apples in a saucepan. Combine sherry, water, orange juice, honey and ginger. Pour over fruit and cook over medium heat for 15-20 minutes. Remove from heat, stir in grapefruit segments and cool to room temperature. Spoon fruit into grapefruit cups to serve.

POTATO AND SALAMI FRITATTA

The fritatta can be partially prepared the night before, covered, refrigerated and baked just before serving. A non-stick pie plate is ideal for this dish.

Serves 10

- [ ] **1 tablespoon olive oil**
- [ ] **1 large potato, thinly sliced**
- [ ] **100 g colbassi sausage (Hungarian sausage), sliced**
- [ ] **1/2 red capsicum, cut into thin strips**
- [ ] **4 shallots, chopped**
- [ ] **2 tablespoons chopped fresh basil**
- [ ] **6 eggs, beaten**
- [ ] **freshly ground black pepper**
- [ ] **4 tablespoons grated tasty cheese**

1   Lightly brush a 23 cm pie plate with oil. Spread potato over base. Cover and bake at 180°C for 30 minutes or until tender.

2   Arrange sausage, capsicum and shallots attractively over potatoes. Sprinkle with basil and pour eggs over top. Season to taste with pepper. Top with cheese and bake at 180°C for 15-20 minutes or until firm. Cool for 10 minutes before cutting into wedges.

MARMALADE MUFFINS

These muffins keep very well, so they can be made two or three days in advance. They can be reheated in the microwave on the day. Six muffins take 1 1/2 to 2 minutes to heat on HIGH (100%).

Makes 12

- [ ] **2 cups (90 g) All-Bran**
- [ ] **1 1/2 cups (375 mL) milk**
- [ ] **125 g butter, melted**
- [ ] **2 eggs, lightly beaten**
- [ ] **2 cups (250 g) self-raising flour, sifted**
- [ ] **2 teaspoons baking powder**
- [ ] **2 teaspoons mixed spice**
- [ ] **1 cup (170 g) brown sugar**
- [ ] **4 tablespoons marmalade**

1 Place bran and milk in a large bowl and set aside until milk is absorbed. Combine butter and eggs and stir into bran mixture.
2 Combine flour, baking powder, mixed spice and sugar and fold into bran mixture. Spoon half the muffin mixture into greased muffin pans. Top with a teaspoon of marmalade then cover with remaining muffin mixture. Bake at 200°C for 20-25 minutes or until well risen and golden brown.

TOMATO AND SPINACH ROULADE

The sauce and filling can be made the day before. Cover the sauce with plastic food-wrap and store in refrigerator. On the day, it is just a matter of completing the preparation and cooking the roulade. Gently reheat the filling before spreading it on the roulade.

Serves 10

- [ ] **60 g butter**
- [ ] **1/2 cup (60 g) plain flour**
- [ ] **2 tablespoons chopped fresh basil**
- [ ] **1/2 cup (125 mL) milk**
- [ ] **1/2 cup (125 mL) light sour cream**
- [ ] **4 eggs, separated**
- [ ] **2 tablespoons tomato paste**
- [ ] **grated Parmesan cheese**

SPINACH FILLING
- [ ] **30 g butter**
- [ ] **1 onion, finely chopped**
- [ ] **8 spinach leaves, stalks removed and shredded**
- [ ] **3 tablespoons toasted pine nuts**
- [ ] **250 g ricotta cheese**
- [ ] **freshly ground black pepper**

1 Melt butter in a saucepan, stir in flour and basil. Cook for 1-2 minutes. Combine milk and sour cream and gradually blend into flour mixture. Cook over medium heat until sauce boils and thickens.
2 Whisk in egg yolks and tomato paste. Transfer mixture to a large bowl. Beat egg whites until stiff peaks form and lightly fold through tomato mixture.
3 Pour into a greased and lined 25 cm x 30 cm Swiss roll pan. Bake at 250°C for 12-15 minutes or until puffed and golden

Marmalade Muffins, Plain and Spinach Pancakes with sweet and savoury fillings, Tomato and Spinach Roulade

brown. Turn out onto a sheet of baking paper sprinkled with Parmesan cheese.

4   To make filling, melt butter in a frypan and cook onion and spinach for 2-3 minutes. Remove from heat and stir in pine nuts and ricotta cheese. Season to taste with pepper. Spread mixture evenly over roulade and gently roll up. Slice roulade to serve.

PANCAKE STACKS

These pancake stacks make great party food, as most of the preparation can be done in advance. Make the pancakes and layer them between sheets of baking paper. When cool, wrap in foil or plastic food wrap and refrigerate or freeze until you are ready to use them. Stack and reheat just before serving. The fillings can be arranged on plates and in bowls early in the day, then covered and refrigerated until needed. All you will have to do is arrange the fillings attractively around the pancake stacks.

PLAIN PANCAKES

Makes 10

- ☐ 1^1/2 cups (190 g) plain flour, sifted
- ☐ 3 eggs, lightly beaten
- ☐ 1 tablespoon polyunsaturated oil
- ☐ 1^1/4 cups milk

1   Place flour in a bowl and make a well in the centre. Add eggs and oil and work flour in from sides. Stir in milk a little at a time to make a smooth batter of pouring consistency.

2   Transfer batter to a jug and stand for 30 minutes before cooking.

3   Pour 2-3 tablespoons of batter into a heated, greased crepe pan. Cook pancakes until golden brown each side.

SPINACH PANCAKES

Makes 10

- ☐ 1 cup (125 g) plain flour, sifted
- ☐ 3 eggs, lightly beaten
- ☐ 1 tablespoon melted butter
- ☐ ^{1}/2 cup (190 mL) milk
- ☐ ^{1}/2 cup (125 mL) buttermilk
- ☐ 250 g frozen chopped spinach, thawed

1   Place flour in a bowl and make a well in the centre. Add eggs, butter, milk and buttermilk. Mix well until combined. Squeeze spinach to remove excess water and stir into batter. Stand for 30 minutes before cooking.

2   Cook as for plain pancakes.

SUGGESTED FILLINGS

We have put together the following fillings as suggestions you might like to try. Just remember to give your guests a variety so that both the sweet and savoury tooth are satisfied.

- ☐ smoked salmon, sour cream and caviar
- ☐ sugar and lemon juice
- ☐ fresh berries and cream
- ☐ avocado slices, lemon juice and ricotta cheese
- ☐ mascarpone cheese and honey
- ☐ homemade jam and cream

CHEESE PASTRY CUPS WITH SALMON SOUFFLE

Make the pastry cases in advance. They will keep in an airtight container for a week or can be frozen for up to a month.

Serves 10

PASTRY
- [ ] **3 cups plain flour, sifted**
- [ ] **185 g butter**
- [ ] **2 tablespoons dried onion flakes**
- [ ] **2$^1/_2$ tablespoons grated Parmesan cheese**
- [ ] **2 tablespoons grated tasty cheese**
- [ ] **1 tablespoon sour cream**
- [ ] **2-3 tablespoons iced water**

SOUFFLE FILLING
- [ ] **60 g butter**
- [ ] **2 tablespoons plain flour**
- [ ] **pinch chilli powder**
- [ ] **2-3 drops tabasco sauce**
- [ ] **220 g can red salmon, drained and liquid reserved**
- [ ] **1 cup milk**
- [ ] **1$^1/_2$ tablespoons mayonnaise**
- [ ] **1$^1/_2$ tablespoons cream**
- [ ] **1 teaspoon lemon juice**
- [ ] **3 egg yolks**
- [ ] **4 egg whites**

1   To make pastry, place flour in a large bowl. Rub in butter until mixture resembles fine breadcrumbs. Stir in onion flakes, Parmesan and tasty cheese. Combine sour cream with water to make a firm dough.

2   Divide pastry into 10 portions. Roll out each portion large enough to line a brioche pan (measuring 9 cm across top). Trim pastry edges and prick base with a fork. Bake at 220°C for 10 minutes. Remove from oven and set aside to cool. Remove pastry cups from brioche pans.

3   For souffle, melt butter in a saucepan. Stir in flour, chilli powder and tabasco. Cook 1-2 minutes over medium heat. Combine reserved liquid and milk, and gradually stir liquid into flour mixture. Cook over medium heat until sauce boils and thickens.

4   Remove pan from heat and stir in salmon, mayonnaise, cream, lemon juice and egg yolks. Beat egg whites until stiff peaks form. Lightly fold through salmon mixture. Spoon souffle mixture into pastry cups. Bake at 180°C for 20-25 minutes or until well puffed and golden on top.

WEDDING FARE WITH FLAIR

WEDDING TIME	SUGGESTED FARE
early morning	breakfast or brunch served indoors or in the garden
mid-morning	cake and champagne
noon wedding	light lunch
early to mid-afternoon	high tea
late afternoon	cocktail party dinner and dance

DILL PIKELETS WITH OYSTERS AND CAVIAR

Prepare pikelets in advance and freeze. On the day, thaw and gently reheat.

Serves 25

- [ ] **1 cup (125 g) plain flour, sifted**
- [ ] **freshly ground black pepper**
- [ ] **$^1/_4$ teaspoon bicarbonate of soda**
- [ ] **1 egg, lightly beaten**
- [ ] **1 cup (250 mL) buttermilk**
- [ ] **2 teaspoons chopped fresh dill**
- [ ] **15 g butter, melted**
- [ ] **extra butter**

TOPPING
- [ ] **25 shelled oysters**
- [ ] **sour cream**
- [ ] **caviar**
- [ ] **dill sprigs**
- [ ] **lemon slices**

1   Place flour, pepper, bicarbonate of soda, egg, buttermilk, dill and melted butter in a food processor or blender and process until smooth.

2   Heat a heavy-based frypan over medium heat. Add a knob of butter. Drop spoonfuls of batter into pan. Cook over medium heat until bubbles appear and burst. Turn pikelets and cook until golden brown on each side. Continue until all the batter is used.

3   Top each pikelet with an oyster and a spoonful of sour cream. Decorate with caviar, dill and lemon slices to serve.

❖ TASTY TOPPINGS ❖

Try topping our dill pikelets with smoked salmon and mayonnaise, turkey and cranberry sauce or grated carrot and orange.

TANGY TOMATO COOLER

This is a real refresher without alcohol.

Serves 10

- [ ] **2 litres tomato juice**
- [ ] **3 teaspoons Worcestershire sauce**
- [ ] **$^1/_4$ teaspoon chilli powder**
- [ ] **1$^1/_2$ teaspoons celery salt**
- [ ] **1 teaspoon grated lemon rind**
- [ ] **$^3/_4$ cup (190 mL) lemon juice**
- [ ] **ice cubes**
- [ ] **celery sticks and lemon slices for garnish**

1   Mix together tomato juice, Worcestershire sauce, chilli powder, celery salt, lemon rind and lemon juice.

2   Place ice cubes in a glass and pour tomato drink over. Garnish with celery sticks and lemon slices.

STRAWBERRY PUNCH

Serves 10

- [ ] **1$^1/_2$ cups (375 g) sugar**
- [ ] **2 cups (500 mL) water**
- [ ] **350 g strawberries**
- [ ] **2 bottles non-alcoholic sparkling white wine, chilled**
- [ ] **$^1/_2$ cup (150 g) mint leaves**

1   Place sugar and water in a large saucepan. Cook over medium heat, stirring constantly until sugar dissolves. Bring to the boil, reduce heat and simmer for 10 minutes. Add 250 g of the strawberries and simmer for 5 minutes. Remove from heat and set aside to cool.

2   Pour strawberry mixture into a food processor or blender and puree. Pour into a shallow cake pan and freeze until set.

3   Flake strawberry mixture into a large punch bowl or jug. Pour in wine and stir to combine. Slice remaining strawberries and float on top of punch with mint leaves.

FRESH BERRY CORNUCOPIA

Make the pastry cornucopia two or three days in advance and store in an airtight container.

Serves 12

- ☐ **500 g prepared puff pastry**
- ☐ **1 egg, lightly beaten**
- ☐ **icing sugar**
- ☐ **quantity mixed berries, such as strawberries, raspberries and blueberries**

1 To make cornucopia, cut a piece of heavy duty aluminium foil about 30 cm x 56 cm. Roll into a cone shape 30 cm long by 15 cm in diameter at the open end. Crumple some greaseproof paper and pack into foil cone to help hold its shape.

2 Roll pastry into a rectangle 25 cm x 60 cm. Cut off a 20 cm piece and cut into strips measuring 25 cm x 1 cm. Place strips 1 cm apart on a sheet of baking paper. Cut remaining pastry into strips measuring 40 cm x 1 cm and weave across first strips to form a tight lattice. Cover pastry with another sheet of baking paper and refrigerate for 15 minutes.

3 Lay chilled pastry lattice on a flat surface. Remove top sheet of baking paper. Place foil mould diagonally across pastry lattice, with open end pointing towards bottom left-hand corner of pastry. Gently fold top left-hand corner of pastry over foil mould towards bottom right corner. Continue to roll mould towards bottom right corner. Trim any loose pastry ends with a sharp knife. With remaining strips of pastry make a plait to fit around open edge of cornucopia. Brush edge of pastry cone with beaten egg. Position pastry plait around open edge of cone and refrigerate for 15 minutes.

4 Brush cornucopia with beaten egg and transfer to a greased oven tray. Bake at 200°C for 20-25 minutes or until golden brown. Remove from oven and cool on a wire rack. Carefully remove foil mould. Dust with icing sugar and fill with berries to serve.

WEDDING BELLES

Choosing the wedding dress is every bride's greatest pleasure and, at the same time, her greatest anxiety. Use our guidelines to make the right choice.

There is a dress style for every kind of figure and once you've analysed your shape, the next step is to select a design and fabric which will best suit you. Your gown will also depend on the type of ceremony you plan to have, the season, your personality and, of course, your budget. For an informal wedding, dresses may be long or graze the calf and a veil or headdress is optional. Add a splash of colour by threading ribbon through your hair or adding colourful trim to your bouquet. Semi-formal wedding gowns are usually floor-length and a fingertip veil is worn. For a formal wedding, romance and ritual is everything and the more opulent and fanciful the dress the better. Traditionally, a formal wedding was an all-white affair, but brides now also wear ivory, and gloves and train are optional. Attendants wear formal dress.

Overtrimming a gown is a common mistake. If you are overweight, lots of frills and bows can make you look even bigger, and if you are petite they can overwhelm you. Brides with broad hips should opt for a gown with a skirt cut on the bias, to highlight more slender parts of the body such as the neck, arms or ankles.

Full-skirted styles are best suited to tall, slender figures

Girls who are tall with full figures should look to simple designs which are neat fitting rather than bouffant or body-hugging.

Once you have a good idea of the style, arrange to have it made if you don't intend to make it yourself, or hire or buy a gown off the rack. A good designer will consider all your features and your colouring and suggest some ideas for the bouquet and accessories to complement the gown. State your budget at the beginning. It shouldn't alter the basic style but it may affect the choice of fabric.

Clever use of fabric can transform a simple style

For brides who are short with a full figure, plain and simply styled gowns are best. Soft-flowing skirts falling from a bodice with a simple neckline are also flattering.

Vertical lines and slim skirts create the illusion of extra height. Short, thin brides should avoid long trains, full sleeves, excessive trim and heavily textured fabrics.

If you are tall and thin, fullness is the key. You can achieve this by adding ruffles and bows, layering your fabric, or keeping the gown simple but in a heavily textured fabric such as embossed satin, taffeta or lace. Full trains look wonderful and long sleeves disguise thin arms.

❖ SWEET TRADITIONS ❖

We are all familiar with the old adage:

Something old,
Something new,
Something borrowed,
Something blue,

but few of us know the last line which goes:

And a silver sixpence in your shoe.

Each phrase represents a superstition important to a bride on her wedding day, and is traditionally represented by an item of clothing or jewellery. _Something old_ represents her past, _something new_ represents her future, _something borrowed_ is to remind her of the support of others, _something blue_ stands as a sign of her faithfulness, and the _silver sixpence_? A wish for her prosperity!

Fabric can make or ruin any outfit and a wedding dress is no exception. Silk, organza, taffeta and lace are timeless and always lovely.

Silk falls gracefully and lace looks rich and extravagant. Satin is sensuous and the lustre will accentuate your curves. Organza is ideal for gowns of a bouffant style, and taffeta flatters most figures. A word of caution however; if you want to use lace with another fabric buy the lace first as it is easier to match the fabric to the lace than the other way around.

If you decide to make your own gown, plan your sewing area carefully. Keep the floor immaculately clean; the area should be well lit with an iron

Slim-skirted styles give an impression of added height

17

close at hand, and plenty of storage space. Never iron directly onto your fabric. Place a damp cloth over the dress before pressing. Protect the delicate fibres of the fabric and ensure it stays clean

Dresses for bridesmaids complement the bride's and are normally the same length but less elaborate in style and fabric. All clothes, flowers and colours should harmonise. A good choice for bridesmaids is a two-piece outfit rather than a dress. Worn together on the day, it can look appropriately formal but afterwards may be worn as a party dress.

❖ **THE SHOE BOX** ❖

Choose a simple style with a heel height appropriate to your size, your fiancé's height, and the style of your dress. White satin court shoes or ballet slippers are traditional for brides and bridesmaids but generally end up as white elephants in the bottom of the wardrobe. A more practical choice is a shoe which you can wear on other occasions. A white leather shoe can be dyed later to suit the rest of your wardrobe.

Pastel colours and floral prints are very popular for bridesmaids (above)

Beautiful ribbons, satin roses and delicate laces are the perfect trims for a wedding outfit – don't forget the shoes when planning these finishing touches

WEDDING GIFT LIST

Compiling a list of gifts you and your husband-to-be would really appreciate is not presumptuous – it is commonsense! Who wants to have to return unwanted toasters, find storage space for six butter dishes and three irons all given by well-intentioned guests? Or find yourself without saucepans, a kettle or bath towels? Making a gift list solves both problems for friends and relatives undecided about what to buy and helps to furnish your home with co-ordinated style.

Large department stores and selected specialty stores operate gift lists at no cost to you. Most stores also allow you to list items which are only available elsewhere. It is best to cover as broad a range of items as possible to allow for your guests' individual pockets and individual tastes. Don't be embarrassed to list larger or more expensive items. Some friends may prefer to pool their resources to buy an expensive gift of lasting value.

It is best to set up your list as soon as your engagement is announced, and you should jointly decide on the items to include.

Look through home-making magazines for inspiration, go window shopping, and consider each room in your house and what is required to furnish them to your liking. It is the perfect opportunity to start a china, silver or crystal collection.

On receipt of presents, send thank you cards. If the goods have guarantees, fill in the forms and return them promptly to the company. Store your presents in their original boxes in a secure place until you are ready to move them into your new home.

MUSICAL NOTES

Strike a joyous note for your wedding with a carefully selected repertoire of hymns, mood music and dance tunes. 'Here Comes the Bride' is synonymous with weddings but you can choose almost any type of music to herald your walk up the aisle so don't be limited by tradition.

Before choosing your music, it is wise to speak with your clergyman and find out if there are any rules which limit your choice. Remember, contemporary pieces may be out of place at a very formal wedding. A choir or organ recital can add a special touch.

Apart from hymns, there are many classic pieces by Mozart, Beethoven, Haydn or Bach which will heighten the sense of occasion. Make music for an outdoor wedding bright and cheery.

Some suggestions for the music to be played while guests await the bride's arrival at the church include: Bach's 'Jesu, Joy of Man's Desiring', or 'In the Hall of the Mountain King', from Grieg's *Peer Gynt Suite*, which build up to the majestic processional march. Wagner's 'Bridal Chorus' is wonderful for when the bridal party moves to the vestry to sign the register, as is Mozart's *Allegro* or an excerpt from Vivaldi's popular concerto *Four Seasons*.

For the recessional march, music should be lively. A perennial favourite is Mendelssohn's 'Wedding March' from *A Midsummer Night's Dream.* You may, of course, choose an appropriate contemporary piece of music if you prefer.

Music for the reception should be bright and incorporate good dance music. There should be a fanfare for the newlyweds' arrival at the reception, and perhaps for the speeches and toasts.

We all like to dance at a wedding. Traditionally, the bride and groom dance the first waltz, and are then joined by their parents, after which all the guests are welcome to join in.

❖ **WRAPPING PRESENTS** ❖
Many a bride and groom have had to play detective to identify gifts which have lost their tags or cards. Remember when your gift is beautifully wrapped to attach your card very securely with tape or ribbon.

PEN TO PAPER

Invitations herald a happy event, and none more so than wedding invitations. Your choice of stationery is personal, and should reflect the type of service you've chosen.

Conventional weddings call for conservative wording and traditional designs. Until recently, such invitations would always have been written in gold or silver on white paper. Today, delicate spring flower motifs on coloured paper are popular.

Wording can differ considerably, but some basic rules are:

❖ A guest's name should be written in full (although you can omit the middle name and use only the initial).

❖ Dates are written in full (you don't have to give the year).

❖ Times are spelled out (for example, five o'clock or half past three) with the phrase 'in the morning' or 'in the afternoon' if you want to make a distinction.

❖ Addresses are written in full with the street number in numerals.

❖ If it is an invitation to the wedding ceremony and reception, use the words 'request the honour of your presence'.

❖ If it is an invitation to the reception only, use the wording 'request the pleasure of your company'.

❖ For a wedding at the reception venue, write the name of the reception venue only.

❖ The return address should be that of the bride's parents whenever possible.

Some couples opt for a quiet family wedding with a reception for all their friends and relatives afterwards. Wording for this should be simple without any mention of the wedding venue. For those friends you wish to invite to the ceremony, enclose an informal handwritten note giving details of time and place.

There are lots of design ideas for invitations. Instead of engraving them, why not have the invitations written in calligraphy? Rather than gilt-edged cards, choose recycled paper which is available in modern colours and in different sized sheets; you can also buy envelopes to match.

Informal invitations are appropriate for weddings of 50 or less guests, a second marriage, a marriage between older people, or if the wedding has been arranged at short notice. Wording for these should be personalised and handwritten by the bride's mother or the bride herself.

Other items to consider when choosing the stationery are: order of service for the church and place cards for the reception. If you have far-off family or friends, send them a piece of wedding cake in a printed cake box.

1   To make deckle, construct two identical frames, like picture frames, the same size as desired size of paper. Take care that top and bottom of deckle are flat. Cover bottom of one frame with muslin or cheesecloth, pulling fabric firmly across frame and slightly up sides. Staple or tack fabric securely into place.
2   Tear up paper scraps into pieces about 4 cm x 4 cm. Place into electric blender with water and reduce to pulp. For calligraphy quality paper, add a little starch to pulp. Pour pulp into rectangular basin.
3   Place open deckle on top of covered deckle so that fabric lies between them. Holding them firmly together, slide deckle through pulp, evenly scooping some of it up. Allow pulp to drain and remove top frame. Flip pulp onto damp kitchen wipe laid across damp towel (called a couch).
4   Make 6 or 7 layers of pulp and kitchen wipes. Place on floor with bread board on

top. Stand on board to squeeze out excess water. Dry each layer of pulp between sheets of newspaper. When pulp is dry peel away kitchen wipes and paper is ready to use.

❖ SHORT AND SWEET ❖

Toasts and speeches are necessary, but keep them short! The bride's father toasts the couple and the groom replies. He thanks the bride's parents and the guests and toasts the bride's attendants. The best man replies on behalf of the bridesmaids and reads out the telegrams from absent friends and family.

❖ A FLORAL TOUCH ❖

To decorate your notepaper with flowers, first press the flowers in a special press or simply use sheets of blotting paper weighted down with heavy books. Then allow the flowers to dry until they feel papery to the touch. When the flowers are dry, glue them to the corners of your handmade notepapers.

❖

HANDMADE PAPER

Handmade paper is the perfect choice for invitations and for writing all those special thank you notes after the wedding.

☐ **paper scraps, not newspaper or thick, glossy magazine paper (remember, strongly coloured paper will produce a coloured result)**
☐ **mould or ("deckle") to shape paper**
☐ **starch (optional)**
☐ **kitchen wipes or squares of calico larger than the deckle**
☐ **electric blender**

Opposite and right: decorate handmade notepaper with dried flowers, leaves and ribbons

INDIVIDUAL STYLE

We all look for a gift that is more personal than the usual shop-bought one. Here are some ideas to give those essential household items your own individual style.

❖

DAINTY TOWELS

Make these beautiful towels for the bride's trousseau with a minimum of effort and cost. Simply purchase a pair of towels or face cloths and stitch on some embroidered and lacy braid in single or double rows for a truly special gift. Take care to choose a cotton trim for ease of washing.

❖

MONOGRAMMED PILLOW CASES

- [ ] **2.5 m of 90 cm white pique or other similar cotton for each pair of pillow cases**
- [ ] **1.5 m printed cotton for border**
- [ ] **about 4 m bias binding**
- [ ] **embroidery thread**

1   For each pillow case cut a rectangle 52 cm x 75 cm out of both fabrics. Cut a rectangle 32 cm x 55 cm out of centre of print rectangle. Cut a piece of white cotton 52 cm x 90 cm for back.

2   Sew print section to its matching white section at one short end, with right side of print section facing wrong side of white section.

3   Turn 1 cm on raw inside edges of print section to wrong side. You will first need to snip 1 cm diagonally into corners. Press folded edges. Turn print section to right side. Topstitch seam.

4   Press bias binding over double and pin under pressed edges of print section, with folded edge protruding as shown. Stitch around inner edges of print section, through all thicknesses, fixing them to white backing and securing bias binding at the same time. From here on treat as a single layer of fabric.

5   Turn under 6 mm and again 1 cm along one short end of white pillow case back. Stitch and press. Place back onto completed front section with right sides together and raw edges even. Note that finished edge of pillow case back extends beyond finished edge of front. Fold this extension over pillow case front, keeping raw side edges even. Stitch front to back along sides and lower edge. Overlock or zigzag raw edges together. Turn and press.

6   Transfer monogram to desired position on front of pillow case, either by tracing it directly or drawing it through carbon paper. Embroider monogram in small chain stitches or satin stitch as preferred.

❖

TRIMMED SHEETS

- [ ] **pair purchased white sheets, only one is trimmed**
- [ ] **strip of trimming fabric 12 cm wide**
- [ ] **bias binding**

1   Hem both short ends of contrast strip. Press. You may have to join strips to achieve desired length. If so, take care to stitch as invisibly as possible and press all seams before proceeding.

2   Place contrast strip on top edge of sheet so that right side of strip faces wrong side of sheet. Stitch along top edge of sheet. Turn trim to right side. Press.

2   Press under 1 cm on raw edge of strip. Press bias binding over double and place under pressed edge of strip so that folded edge protrudes as shown. Stitch edge down through all thicknesses, fixing bias binding into place at same time.

3   Topstitch sides of contrast strip in line with stitching on sheet.

Above: Dainty Towels; right: Monogrammed Pillow Cases

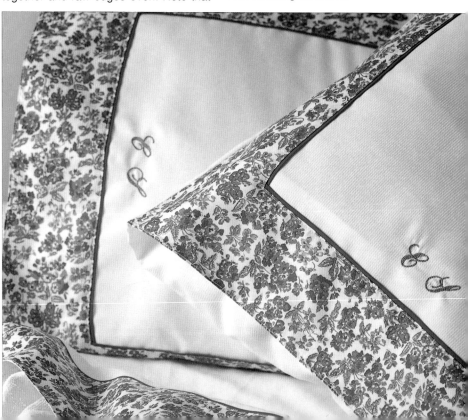

PERSONAL
TOUCHES

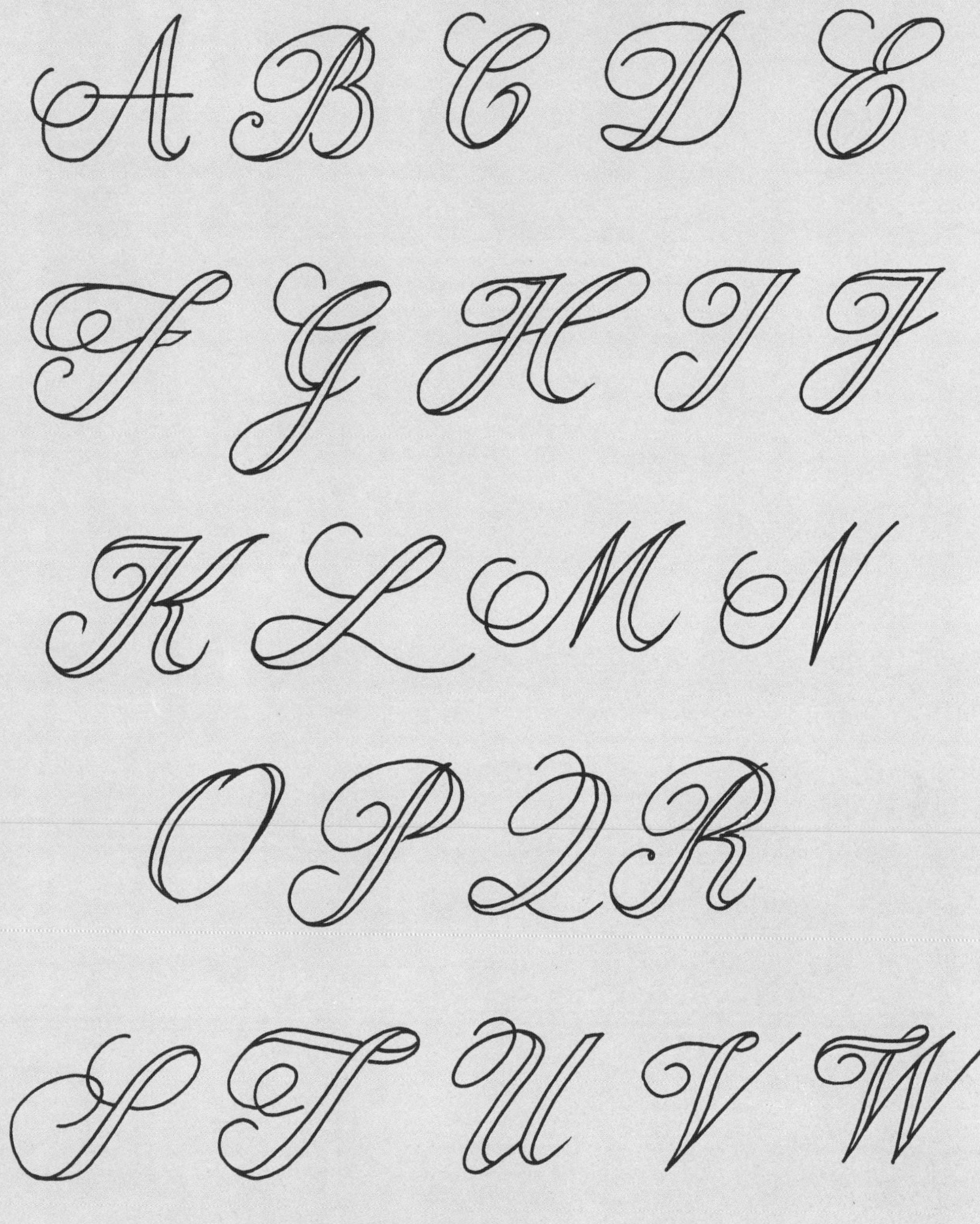

A B C D E

F G H I J

K L M N

O P Q R

S T U V W

X Y Z

PLACE MATS

These quilted and trimmed paisley place mats will grace the newlyweds' table. Make the napkins in the same fabric.

For each place mat:
- ☐ **90 cm wide cotton print fabric**
- ☐ **50 cm x 35 cm polyester wadding**
- ☐ **bias binding**

1   Cut out one piece of fabric 50 cm x 35 cm and another 72 cm x 57 cm for back and front border.

2   Baste wadding onto wrong side of smaller piece of fabric. Lay larger piece wrong side up with smaller piece in position on top with right side up. Fold in edges of larger fabric piece. Pin and press in fullness at corners to mark lines for mitred corners. Cut away this excess fabric leaving a 1 cm seam allowance. Stitch corner seams up to 1 cm from inner edge. Turn and press. Press in raw edge all around border.

3   Press bias binding over double. Place bias binding under pressed inner edges of border so that folded edge protrudes as shown. Stitch through all thicknesses.

NAPKINS

Printed cotton napkins with attractively mitred corners complement your paisley place mats.

For each napkin:
- ☐ **one square of fabric 44 cm x 44 cm and four more strips each 9 cm x 44 cm**
- ☐ **bias binding**

1   Sew strips together to form squared border, mitring corners. Trim away excess fabric. Press. Place right side of border

against wrong side of fa_..ic square with raw edges even. Stitch around outside edges. Trim seams. Turn border to right side. Press. Topstitch.

2   Turn in 1 cm on inner raw edges of border. You will first need to clip 1 cm diagonally into corners. Press.

3   Press bias binding over double. Place bias binding under pressed edge of border so that folded edge protrudes as shown. Stitch through all thicknesses.

❖

CORK MATS

A practical cork mat can become a very pretty one with a little paint and imagination. You will see that we have painted our mats with a motif from the place mat and napkin fabric using acrylic paints. If you are less confident of your artistic skills, try painting a simple geometric motif or a simple flower outline. Make napkins and place mats in a fabric to match your motif.

❖

BEAUTIFUL BOXES

For an unusual and very lovely gift, cover and trim a beautiful box to hold pearls and gloves or hats and scarves. As well as being very useful they will add a decorator's touch to any room.

❖

FLORAL HAT BOX

- ☐ **cardboard or balsawood box**
- ☐ **floral cotton fabric to cover**
- ☐ **cotton lace, finished on both edges**
- ☐ **thin polyester wadding**
- ☐ **craft glue**

1   Allow 1 cm around all cutting edges for turning, as required.

2   Using lid as template, cut out three circles from fabric, allowing an extra 1 cm all around. Cut a strip of fabric to cover sides of box, inside and out, and as long as box in circumference. Cut another strip to cover side of lid and as long as circumference of lid.

3   Cover box with wadding as for lace-covered box on page 41.

4   Cover box with fabric as for lining of lace-covered box.

5   Glue lace over raw edge of fabric on inside of box and lid.

❖ **WITH THIS RING** ❖

The wedding ring tradition dates back to an ancient belief that a vein ran straight from the third finger to the heart. A Greek bride wears her betrothal ring on her left hand until her wedding when it is moved to her right.

Opposite: matching place mats, napkins and hand-painted cork mats below: fabric-covered boxes are both pretty and practical

FOR THE
FLOWER GIRL

*The perfect gift for the flower girl is a charming white
mouse, dressed just as she is! Remember to add the circlet
of flowers about the mouse's ears.*

❖ A WEDDING MOUSE

*If your flower girl is under three years of
age, it would be wise to omit the pearl
necklace and embroider the eyes.*

- ☐ **30 cm felt**
- ☐ **2 small pearl beads for eyes**
- ☐ **polyester wadding**
- ☐ **scraps pretty floral fabric**
- ☐ **string of pearls**

1 Enlarge pattern pieces to actual size.
Each square is 2.5 cm x 2.5 cm (1 inch x
1 inch). Cut out pattern pieces as directed.
6 mm seam allowed all around. Clip all
curved seam allowances for ease. Join all
pieces with right sides facing.

2 Place feet sections together two by
two. Sew around curved edge. Clip seam
and turn. Stuff firmly, leaving area at
straight edge free for stitching. Handsew a
running stitch across opening. Pull up
thread slightly.

3 Place body sections together. Leaving
opening for tail, stitch from centre back,
around nose and down centre front body.

4 Fold tail in half lengthways. Stitch edges
together with small zigzag stitches. Do not
turn. Stuff firmly. Insert tail into opening in
centre back with raw edges even. Stitch
over opening, securing tail.

5 Sew base to lower edge of mouse,
leaving opening for turning. Clip seam,
turn and stuff firmly. Close opening by
hand.

6 Position feet as shown and handsew
into place.

7 Place ear sections together two by
two. Stitch around curved edge. Turn and
stuff lightly. Fold lower corners to centre.
Stitch across straight edge by hand. Draw
up thread to gather slightly. Attach ears at
points marked.

*A white felt mouse in her wedding outfit
will delight the flower girl*

8 Place arm sections together two by
two. Sew around curved edge. Turn and
stuff firmly. Close opening by hand. Attach
arms to body.

9 Sew on eyes, pulling thread firmly from
one side of head to the other to contour
face. Draw buttonhole thread several times
through nose for whiskers.

Our wedding mouse is dressed in a profu-
sion of frills. Make a number of fabric frills
and attach to mouse with the narrowest at
the neck and widest at the hem. Tie a
fabric bow around her waist. For her floral
headdress we joined a number of ribbon
roses and sewed them around her ears as
illustrated. A string of pearls gives the
perfect finishing touch.

❖ WHO'S NEXT? ❖

Throwing the bouquet origi-
nated in America in the late
1800s. A bride sometimes
carried as many small bouquets as she had bridesmaids,
one of them containing a
ring. As the bride left the
church she threw her bou-
quets to her bridesmaids.
Whoever caught the bouquet
was thought to be
the next bride.

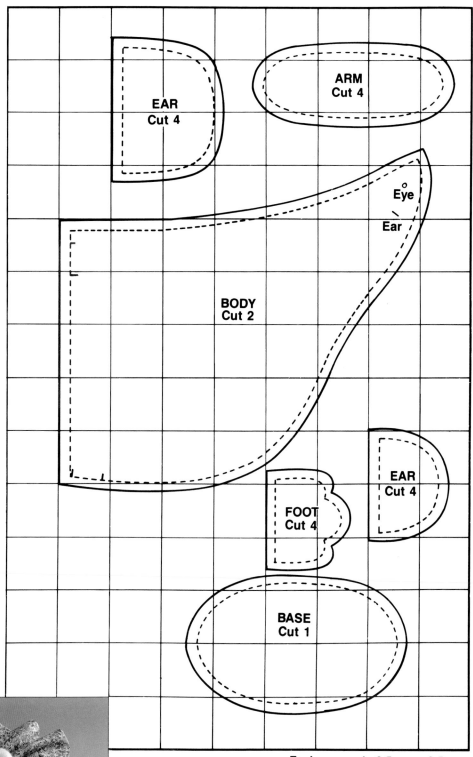

EAR
Cut 4

ARM
Cut 4

Eye

Ear

BODY
Cut 2

EAR
Cut 4

FOOT
Cut 4

BASE
Cut 1

Each square is 2.5 cm x 2.5 cm.

BRIMMING
BASKETS

A beautiful basket, trimmed and filled with pretty and practical items for the home, makes a wonderful gift. Choose a basket that will best suit the bride and groom, such as a kitchen basket for keen cooks or a garden basket for those with green fingers.

BATHROOM BASKET

- [ ] **shallow cane basket with handle**
- [ ] **pretty cotton print fabric**
- [ ] **iron-on interfacing**
- [ ] **bathroom items for filling basket**

1 Allow 1 cm for seams all around. Cut out a circle of fabric to cover base of basket and another to cover side of basket to lip. Interface both these pieces. Cut a frill twice as long as circumference of basket and as wide as twice the distance from lip of basket to desired length of frill.

2 Sew base cover to side cover. Place inside basket. Mark position and width of handles.

3 Divide fabric strip for frill into two. Press in raw edges at ends. Fold frills over double. Gather raw edges. Sew another two rows of gathering on outside just below level of basket lip.

3 Sew frills to liner, on either side of handles, drawing up inner gathering to fit. Position complete liner in basket and draw up outer gathering to fit.

4 Cut strip of fabric twice length of handle and as wide as circumference of handle plus 4 cm. Press in 1 cm on long raw edges. Fold over double with wrong sides together. Sew a gathering thread along fold and separate gathering threads along each of pressed edges. Draw up gathering on fold and place cover around handle. Draw up other gathering to fit. Handsew gathered edges together, through gathering stitches. Secure handle covering to liner with small stitches.

5 Cut two strips of fabric, each 80 cm x 20 cm for bows. Cut ends off at an angle. Fold over double. Sew around edges, leaving a small opening for turning. Turn and press. Close opening by hand. Tie bows at each end of handle.

6 Fill basket with bathroom goodies such as trimmed towels, loofah, soap, bath oils, talc and so on.

Left: the bathroom gift basket filled with trimmed towels, soaps, bath sponge and loofah

FLORAL BATH FRESHENER

Make a bottle of delightful scented bath freshener and another of luxurious bath oil to include in your bathroom basket.

- ☐ **600 mL (1 pint) petals of roses, cornflowers, violets, lavender, lilac, freesias or other scented flowers**
- ☐ **600 mL (1 pint) white wine vinegar**
- ☐ **300 mL (1/2 pint) water**

1   Fill suitable jars or bottles with rose, violet or other suitable petals.
2   Mix vinegar and water and heat mixture until just boiling. Pour over flower petals in bottle.
3   Close bottle and leave in a warm spot for 3-4 weeks. Agitate contents of bottle every day.
4   Strain contents through muslin into a suitable bottle. If you wish, you can strengthen the scent by repeating the process using fresh flowers.

FLORAL BATH OIL

- ☐ **175 mL glycerine**
- ☐ **50 mL floral oil of your choice, such as rose, lavender and violet**

1   Whisk ingredients together until well mixed.
2   Pour into suitable bottle.
3   Label bottle with type of flower used and instruction to add one teaspoon to a hot bath.

KITCHEN BASKET

Fill a white wicker basket with useful kitchen utensils, a pretty tablecloth and matching napkins, a pair of cups and saucers and some delicious homemade preserves (see recipes on pages 30–31). To make the tablecloth, simply hem the edges of a 90 cm x 90 cm square of cotton fabric and sew napkins to match, following the instructions on page 24. Add a generous bow made from remnants of the tablecloth fabric.

Right: the kitchen basket with mugs, spoons, preserves and napkins

GARDEN BASKET

This 'basket' is actually a wonderful terra-cotta pot filled to the brim with useful gifts for the gardener. Include such items as gloves, trowel, packets of seeds, pot plant decorations, clay herb markers, a sun hat and a very smart gardener's apron.

GARDENER'S APRON

- ☐ **two rectangles fabric, each 40 cm x 30 cm, one piece 40 cm x 40 cm for pocket and one strip 150 cm x 10 cm for waistband**
- ☐ **two D-shaped rings**

1   Fold pocket section over double and place on right side of one main piece, with lower raw edges even and folded edge of pocket uppermost.
2   Place second main piece on top of other with right sides together. Round off lower corners of all pieces. Stitch around sides and lower edge, through all thicknesses, leaving top edge open. Turn and press. Stitch down through centre of pocket, dividing it into two.
3   Press in 1 cm on all raw edges of waistband. Place apron between pressed edges at centre of waistband. Stitch all around waistband, securing apron.

Above: the garden basket containing tools, gloves and gardener's apron

PANTRY TREATS

*In a pickle deciding what to give the bride to stock her pantry?
Homemade jams, sauces, and vinegars in attractive jars
are a delectable solution.*

MIDSUMMER NIGHT'S JAM

This pretty jam can be made using any mixture of berries. We used strawberries, raspberries and boysenberries.

Makes 3 medium (375 mL) jars

- ☐ **800 g mixed berries**
- ☐ **1 cup (250 mL) water**
- ☐ **800 g sugar**
- ☐ **juice 1 lemon**

1   Place berries and water in a large saucepan and cook over medium heat for 15 minutes or until fruit softens.
2   Add sugar and lemon juice, stirring constantly until sugar dissolves. Bring berry mixture to the boil and simmer for 20-25 minutes or until jam gels when tested on a cold saucer.
3   Stand for 10 minutes, then pour into hot sterilised jars. Seal when cold.

HERB VINEGARS

Flavoured vinegars make wonderful gifts which add extra zest to any savoury dish, pickle or salad that calls for vinegar. Use fresh herbs such as basil, tarragon, thyme or rosemary. For something different, you might like to use red or white wine vinegar.

Makes 4 cups (1 litre)

- ☐ **2 cups fresh herbs**
- ☐ **4 cups (1 litre) vinegar**

1   Wash the herbs and pat dry. Crush slightly.
2   Place herbs in a bottle and pour over vinegar. Seal and leave in a warm place like a sunny windowsill for 3-4 weeks.
3   Strain vinegar through muslin. Place a fresh herb sprig in a pretty, clean bottle and add vinegar. Seal and label.

BEETROOT, ORANGE AND APPLE CHUTNEY

This chutney is delicious with cheese and cold lamb.

Makes 4 medium (375 mL) jars

- ☐ **1 kg beetroot, stems and leaves removed**
- ☐ **1 cup (250 g) sugar**
- ☐ **1 onion, finely chopped**
- ☐ **2 cups (500 mL) red wine vinegar**
- ☐ **1 teaspoon ground allspice**
- ☐ **2 large Granny Smith apples, peeled and chopped**
- ☐ **1 orange, segmented**

1   Place beetroot in a large saucepan and cover with water. Cover pan and bring to the boil. Reduce heat and simmer for approximately 1 hour or until tender. Drain and set aside to cool slightly. Peel and dice.
2   Combine sugar, onion, vinegar and allspice in a saucepan. Cook over medium

> **❖ PRESERVING TIPS ❖**
> When giving unusual preserves it is a practical idea to tie an attractive label around the neck of the jar with serving suggestions. As an extra to your preserves gift you might like to include the recipe. This could either be on a label around the neck of the jar or written on pretty paper and placed in an envelope to go with the preserves.

30

heat without boiling, stirring constantly until sugar dissolves.

3 Bring mixture to the boil. Reduce heat, add apple and simmer for 15-20 minutes or until apple pulps. Stir in beetroot and orange and cook for 5 minutes longer. Pour into hot sterilised jars and seal when cold.

❖

PICKLED CAPSICUMS

Try our pickled capsicums – they're great served with cold meat.

Makes 1 large (500 mL) jar

- ☐ **2 onions, sliced**
- ☐ **2 red capsicums, sliced**
- ☐ **2 green capsicums, sliced**
- ☐ **2 yellow capsicums, sliced**
- ☐ **2 tablespoons coarse cooking salt**
- ☐ **1 red chilli, finely chopped**
- ☐ **2 bay leaves**
- ☐ **1^1/$_2$ cups (375 mL) white wine vinegar**
- ☐ **1 teaspoon black mustard seeds**
- ☐ **2 teaspoons pink peppercorns**
- ☐ **^{3}/$_4$ cup (185 g) sugar**

1 Combine onions, capsicums and salt in large bowl. Cover and let stand overnight.

2 Rinse vegetables under cold running water. Drain and pat dry on absorbent paper. Arrange attractively in a sterilised jar with the red chilli and bay leaves.

3 Combine vinegar, mustard seeds, peppercorns and sugar in a saucepan. Cook over medium heat without boiling, stirring constantly until sugar dissolves. Bring to the boil, then reduce heat and simmer, uncovered, for 3 minutes. Pour over vegetables in jars and seal while hot.

Herb vinegar looks wonderful in an unusual bottle

❖ PANTRY BASKET ❖

Put together the ingredients of a basic pantry. Assemble them attractively in a pretty basket. You could include canned asparagus, baked beans, baking powder, bicarbonate of soda, chilli sauce, cocoa, coconut, coffee, canned corn kernels, creamed corn, cream of tartar, plain flour, self-raising flour, canned fruits, dried fruits, gelatine, golden syrup, honey, mustards, nuts, pasta, peanut butter, oils, rice, wild rice, canned salmon, soy sauce, canned spaghetti, sugars, tabasco sauce, tea, canned tomatoes, tomato paste, tomato sauce, canned tuna, vinegars, Worcestershire sauce, biscuits, chocolate bars and other treats. This is also a good idea for a group to give the bride, as each can contribute one or two items to the basket.

SILKY SATIN COAT HANGERS

These two hangers are both made to the same instructions, one is trimmed with a satin bow while the other has a heart-shaped sachet attached to the hook.

- ☐ **wooden coat hanger**
- ☐ **piece of silk satin about 1 m x 50 cm**
- ☐ **polyester wadding**
- ☐ **2 mm wide satin ribbon**
- ☐ **1 m gathered lace**
- ☐ **cardboard**
- ☐ **scrap of tulle**
- ☐ **lavender or potpourri**
- ☐ **clear-drying craft glue**

1 Cover coat hanger with wadding. Stitch to secure.

2 Cut two pieces of fabric, each twice the length of hanger and as wide as hanger plus 6 cm. Press in 1.5 cm on all edges. Stitch a gathering thread 1.5 cm from pressed edges.

3 Handsew short ends closed with tiny stitches.

4 Draw up gathering thread around outside edge to almost fit hanger. Slip hanger into cover. Complete drawing up of gathering to fit.

5 Stitch through gathering with small stitches to secure edges, inserting lace in lower edge as you go.

6 Cover hook with buttonhole stitch, using narrow satin ribbon. Secure hook cover to hanger with small stitches.

7 Cut heart shape out of cardboard. Cut out two heart shapes from satin, one 1 cm smaller and one 1 cm larger than cardboard shape. Glue large satin heart to outside, snipping into curves and glueing excess fabric onto other side. Glue small satin heart to inside, covering raw edges. Glue heart-shaped tulle over top, leaving small opening for inserting potpourri. Insert loop for hanging heart into opening. Glue opening closed. Glue gathered lace around edge.

8 Suspend heart from hook. Decorate with bow.

THE BRIDE

EMBROIDERED
LINGERIE BAG

*Grub rose embroidered organza makes
this glamorous bag for packing the honeymoon trousseau.*

- [ ] **two pieces organza, each 40 cm
  x 28 cm**
- [ ] **narrow satin ribbon**
- [ ] **embroidery thread**

1 Sew front and back together, using
French seams. Turn and press.
2 Turn in 6 mm at top edge and turn
again 6 cm.
3 Mark position for buttonholes in centre
front casing. Make two vertical buttonholes by hand in outer layer of casing.
4 Stitch casing into place. Thread ribbon
through casing.
5 Embroider grub roses as shown, following instructions in How To Embroider
Grub Roses on page 37.

THE RING PILLOW

*The best man won't have to worry about losing the ring
when it sits, tied with satin ribbon, on this beautiful pillow
and is carried down the aisle by a charming page boy.*

*This lovely ring pillow can be made for
one ring or two, depending on the type
of ceremony the bridal couple
have chosen*

RING PILLOW

- [ ] **one square of silk voile 1 cm bigger than the pillow insert all around for front; two pieces each half size of front plus 1 cm all around for cushion back**
- [ ] **one square of silk satin for backing**
- [ ] **strip of 18 cm wide lace x twice the circumference of the pillow**
- [ ] **satin piping**
- [ ] **25 cm zipper**
- [ ] **pillow insert about 30 cm square**
- [ ] **narrow satin ribbon**
- [ ] **about 2.5 m insertion lace**

1   Stitch lace onto front panel of pillow as shown. Snip fabric from behind lace.
2   Place right side of satin backing against wrong side of front panel. Baste.
3   Sew piping around edge of right side of lace-trimmed panel with raw edges even.
3   Gather lace and stitch around trimmed panel, matching raw edges.
4   Sew ends of pillow centre back seam, leaving opening for zipper. Insert zipper. Press.
6   Place pillow front and back together with right sides facing. Stitch together along piping stitchline. Turn through zipper opening. Press.
7   Cut two 50 cm lengths of satin ribbon. Handsew centre of each ribbon to pillow front with tiny stitches. Tie rings to pillow.

FLORAL COAT HANGER

- [ ] **wooden coat hanger**
- [ ] **four pieces of voile, each twice length of hanger and as wide as hanger plus 5 cm**
- [ ] **thick polyester wadding**

1 Cover coat hanger thickly with wadding. Stitch to secure.
2 Place fabric pieces together two by two with right sides facing. Stitch around outside edge, leaving opening for turning. Trim seam, turn and press.
3 Sew front to back cover with machine gathering stitches, leaving about 18 cm open at centre top. Gather separately both edges of this opening.
4 Slip hanger into cover one end at a time. Draw up outside gathering to fit. Draw up centre top gathering. Secure both with small stitches.
5 Cut small piece of fabric twice as long as hook and wide enough to go around it plus 1.5 cm. Fold over double with right sides together. Stitch one short and one long side in 6 mm seam. Turn and press. Gather both long sides. Draw cover over hook, pulling up gathering to fit. Stitch to secure.
6 Trim with rouleau bow stitched through to wadding.

SCENTED SHOE STUFFERS

- [ ] **four rectangles of voile each 24 cm x 12 cm, strip for frills 5 cm x 168 cm**
- [ ] **lavender or potpourri**

1 Round off lower corners of all pieces to create toe-shaped end.
2 Cut length of strip in half. Fold over double. Gather raw edges together. Press. Beginning 7 cm from top edge and with raw edges even, sew frill around right side of one fabric piece, ending 7 cm from top edge. Note that frill is curved away at beginning and end to disappear into seam.
3 Place second piece on top of first with right sides together. Stitch together through previous stitching. Turn and press. Fold 7 cm at top edge to inside. Stitch and press.
4 Fill with potpourri or lavender.
5 Tie bow from rouleau or narrow satin ribbon around throat to secure.

Floral Coat Hanger, Scented Shoe Stuffers

SLEEP PILLOW

Fill this pretty pillow with wonderful scents and relaxing herbs to hang from the bed post or slip under the pillow.

- ☐ cut two hearts from floral fabric, one 24 cm x 24 cm and the other 12 cm x 12 cm; cut one heart 24 cm x 24 cm from see-through fabric such as organza
- ☐ strip for ruffle 6 cm x 230 cm
- ☐ scraps for rouleau tie and loop
- ☐ dried flowers, such as lavender, geranium, hops and herbs associated with relaxation, such as rosemary and chamomile

1   Fold strip for ruffles over double with right sides together. Pleat raw edges by hand or with machine ruffle attachment.

2   Sew ruffle to right side of both floral hearts with raw edges even. Turn in raw edges on smaller heart and stitch onto organza heart, stitching in ruffle seamline.

3   Place floral and organza hearts together with right sides facing. Stitch around outside edge, leaving small opening for turning. Trim seam, clipping into curves, turn and press.

4   Fill with flowers or herbs or a mixture of both. Close opening by hand.

5   Make rouleau bow and loop from scraps. Attach to pillow to hang as shown.

FLORAL JEWELLERY BUNDLE

- ☐ two circles of voile 44 cm in diameter and two 32 cm in diameter; two strips each 5 cm wide and twice the length of circumference of circles
- ☐ 150 cm rouleau or narrow satin ribbon

1   Fold each strip for frills over double with wrong sides together. Press. Gather raw edges. Sew frills to right side of one large and one small circle, keeping raw edges even.

2   Place second circle over first with right sides together. Stitch through previous stitching, leaving small opening for turning. Turn and press.

3   Place small circle on large one, matching centres. Stitch four times through centre of small circle, dividing it into eight compartments. Take care to secure beginnings and ends of seams.

4   Stitch casing 4 cm from outer frilled edge. Make two buttonholes by hand on outer layer, between casing lines. Insert rouleau or ribbon. Draw up into bundle.

Sleep Pillow, Floral Jewellery Bundle

LACE-COVERED BOX

- [ ] balsa wood or cardboard oval box about 18 cm x 26 cm
- [ ] remnants of fabric for lining lace, for a truly luxurious effect we used pink silk taffeta
- [ ] 150 cm of 20 cm wide lace, scalloped on both sides
- [ ] thin polyester wadding
- [ ] 1.5 mm wide cream satin ribbon
- [ ] three cream satin ribbon roses
- [ ] clear-drying craft glue

1   Using lid as a template cut out three oval shapes from lining fabric, allowing an extra 1 cm all around. Cut a strip of lining 20 cm x 75 cm for outside of box and another 6 cm x 75 cm for side of lid.

2   With lid in place, pencil a line on box around lower edge of lid. Do not glue any wadding above this line. Glue wadding around outside of box, including base and around lid.

3   Glue one oval inside box on base. Position other oval on outside base. Secure side edge to wadding with small stitches.

4   Press in 1 cm on one long edge of fabric strip. Position strip around side of box so that pressed edge covers raw edge of fabric at lower edge of box. Catch pressed edge into place with small stitches. Fold in raw end and slipstitch into place over other end. Take fabric up side of box, over lip and down into base of box. Mark cutting line on fabric by pressing it into crease where base joins side. Cut away excess fabric and glue edge down.

5   Position lace around side of box so that scalloped edge reaches almost to base. Secure edge to box with small stitches. Turn in raw edge at end of lace and stitch it into place. Take lace up side of box, over lip, and down into box. Glue scalloped edge into place, covering raw edges of fabric. Glue 1.5 mm satin ribbon around outside of box as shown.

6   Position oval of fabric on outside lid. Stitch edge into place on side of lid. Press in raw edge on one long side of narrow strip. Position strip around side of lid with pressed edge over raw edge of fabric. Stitch pressed edge into place. Fold in raw edges at end and secure with small stitches. Take fabric around lip of lid to inside base. Glue edge into place. Glue a length of lace over raw edge if desired.

7   Position lace around lid so that scalloped edge reaches to lip. Fold in raw ends and secure all edges with small stitches. Gather lace into rosette shape at centre. Stitch to secure. Decorate with roses and bows (see page 61). Glue 1.5 mm ribbon around side of lid as for box.

BONBONS

Beautiful bonbons, filled with potpourri or lavender are so simple to make. Why not make a simple lavender bag from the same lace for a pretty set.

- [ ] 16 cm double-edged scalloped lace about 20 cm wide
- [ ] tulle for lining in same size
- [ ] ribbon for trimming
- [ ] potpourri or desired filling

1   Sew raw edges of lace together to form tube. If lining is to be used, place both fabrics together before sewing and treat as single layer.

2   Tie bow around one end.

3   Fill with potpourri and tie bow around other end.

THE WEDDING
CAKE

A slice of happiness is guaranteed for each and every guest with these three wedding cakes. It's the decoration which whets the appetite and recreates the memory.

TRADITIONAL CAKE

- [ ] 250 g raisins, chopped
- [ ] 125 g glace cherries, chopped
- [ ] 500 g sultanas
- [ ] 250 g currants
- [ ] 125 g mixed peel
- [ ] 1 teaspoon grated lemon rind
- [ ] $^1/_2$ cup (125 mL) brandy
- [ ] 250 g butter
- [ ] 1$^1/_2$ cups (250 g) brown sugar
- [ ] 4 eggs
- [ ] 1 tablespoon marmalade
- [ ] 1 tablespoon golden syrup
- [ ] 2 teaspoons glycerine
- [ ] 3 cups (375 g) flour
- [ ] 1 teaspoon mixed spice
- [ ] 1 teaspoon cinnamon
- [ ] 4 tablespoons extra brandy

1 In a large bowl combine raisins, cherries, sultanas, currants, mixed peel, lemon rind and brandy. Cover and stand for 2-3 days, stirring from time to time.

2 Cream butter until light and fluffy. Add brown sugar and beat until just combined. Beat in eggs one at a time. Mix in marmalade, syrup and glycerine.

3 Sift together flour, mixed spice and cinnamon. Stir into creamed mixture alternately with marinated fruit.

4 Spoon cake mixture into prepared pan, making sure that mixture goes right into corners, to give cooked cake a good shape. Wet your hand and smooth top of cake. To eliminate air bubbles, lift cake pan 25 cm above bench top and drop sharply.

5 Bake at 140°C for 3$^1/_2$-4 hours or until cooked when tested. Remove from oven and spoon over extra brandy. Wrap cake in pan with aluminium foil and a thick towel. Leave tightly wrapped until cold.

MARZIPAN PASTE

- [ ] **125 g marzipan meal**
- [ ] **500 g pure icing sugar, sifted**
- [ ] **2 egg yolks**
- [ ] **2 tablespoons lemon juice**
- [ ] **1 tablespoon glycerine**
- [ ] **1 tablespoon sweet sherry**
- [ ] **1-2 drops almond essence, optional**

1 Place marzipan meal and icing sugar in a bowl and mix to combine.
2 In a small bowl, beat together egg yolks, lemon juice, glycerine, sherry and essence. Make a well in centre of dry ingredients and stir in egg mixture.
3 Turn out and knead until smooth and pliable. If the mixture is too soft, knead in a little extra icing sugar and if too dry, knead in a little extra sherry.

COVERING FONDANT

This amount of fondant will cover a 20 cm round or a 20 cm square cake.

- [ ] **3 tablespoons cold water**
- [ ] **1 tablespoon gelatine**
- [ ] **$^1/_2$ cup (125 mL) liquid glucose**
- [ ] **1 tablespoon glycerine**
- [ ] **1 kg pure icing sugar, sifted**

1 Place water in a heatproof bowl. Sprinkle over gelatine, stir and stand for 10 minutes.
2 Place bowl over a pan of very hot water and dissolve gelatine. Add glucose and glycerine and stir well. Remove bowl from pan and set aside to cool slightly.
3 Place 750 g icing sugar in a large bowl. Make a well in the centre and pour in gelatine mixture. Stir into the icing sugar, drawing from the sides until a firm paste is formed. Turn out and knead until smooth and pliable. Place the fondant in a plastic bag and leave at room temperature for at least 24 hours.
4 Turn out and knead in remaining icing sugar. Roll out to a size that is large enough to cover the cake. Place over cake, trimming off excess with a knife.

❖ PREPARING THE CAKE ❖

1 To achieve good evenly shaped cakes, line cake pans with heavy duty aluminium foil, placing shiny side against pan and dull side against cake. Cut three strips of newspaper 2.5 cm wider than sides of cake pan. Position strips around cake pan and secure with string. This acts as an insulator preventing outside edge of cakes from burning.
2 Invert cake onto covered board. Fill any fruit holes or creases in cake with small pieces of marzipan and smooth out with a spatula. Brush cake with beaten egg white. Roll out remaining marzipan and place over cake smoothing sides. Trim away excess. Brush with egg white.
3 Roll out fondant to fit cake size and lift onto cake. Smooth out and trim excess fondant from cake base.
4 To assemble cakes, mark positions for pillars on top of larger cake. Insert thick wooden skewers right through cake to board. Place pillars over skewers and position top cake tier.

MAKING THE FLOWERS

Make one type and colour of flower at a time, so that you will have the same colour and texture for all your flowers. Take the amount of prepared modelling paste you will require and knead in extra icing sugar to make a paste of plasticine consistency. Work in colour if desired. Keep remaining paste in an airtight container and thicken and use as required.

1   To make leaves, form a small teardrop with a little amount of modelling paste. Insert a dampened wire into the centre. Roll over wire and paste, leaving centre part thicker than outer edges. Press out leaf shape using metal leaf cutter. Curve leaves and set aside to dry.

2   To make flowers, make a small teardrop shape using a little modelling paste. Insert a hooked wire through centre and firm paste around base. Gently pull top third of bud with fingertips to form a small flag. Wrap around the bud to represent first petal. Set aside to dry.

3   Roll out modelling paste as thin as possible and cut out shape using a fine petal metal blossom cutter. Flute edges lightly using a wooden toothpick.

4   Remove two petals and wind tightly around dried bud. Moisten base of remaining three petals and attach to base of flower. Turn back petals. Set aside to dry.

5   Cut another blossom round. Flute edges lightly as before. Dampen centre and attach to dried flower. Turn outer petals back.

6   Cut calyx with a cutter and attach to base of flower. Colour flower and calyx as desired with food colouring or powdered chalk.

7   To make flower sprays, assemble flowers using buds, full blown flowers, leaves and ribbon loops to form the desired shape to suit the chosen cake.

MODELLING PASTE

- [ ] **1¹/₂ tablespoons cold water**
- [ ] **2 teaspoons gelatine**
- [ ] **1 teaspoon liquid glucose**
- [ ] **150 g icing sugar, sifted**
- [ ] **extra icing sugar**

1   Place water in a heatproof bowl. Sprinkle over gelatine, stir and stand for 10 minutes.

2   Place bowl over a pan of hot water and dissolve gelatine. Stir in glucose. Remove bowl from pan and set aside to cool slightly. Mix in sifted icing sugar a little at a time, stirring until well combined. Place in an airtight container and leave at room temperature for at least 24 hours before using to make flowers or other decorations for the top of the cake.

WEDDING CAKE CHART

CAKE SIZE	125 g ($^1/_4$ lb)	250 g ($^1/_2$ lb)	375 g ($^3/_4$ lb)	500 g (1 lb)	625 g (1 $^1/_4$ lb)	750 g (1$^1/_2$ lb)
sultanas	250 g	500 g	750 g	1 kg	1.25 kg	1.5 kg
raisins	125 g	250 g	375 g	500 g	625 g	750 g
currants	125 g	250 g	375 g	500 g	625 g	750 g
mixed peel	60 g	125 g	185 g	250 g	300 g	375 g
glace cherries	60 g	125 g	185 g	250 g	300 g	375 g
grated lemon rind	1 tsp	1 tsp	1 tsp	2 tsps	3 tsps	3 tsps
brandy, sherry	60 mL	125 mL	190 mL	250 mL	310 mL	375 mL
butter	125 g	250 g	375 g	500 g	625 g	750 g
brown sugar	125 g	250 g	375 g	500 g	625 g	750 g
eggs	2	4	6	8	10	12
marmalade	2 tsps	1 tbsp	1 $^1/_2$ tbsps	2 tbsps	2 $^1/_2$ tbsps	3 tbsps
golden syrup	2 tsps	1 tbsp	1 $^1/_2$ tbsps	2 tbsps	2 $^1/_2$ tbsps	3 tbsps
glycerine	1 tsp	2 tsps	3 tsps	1 tbsp	1$^1/_4$ tbsp	1$^1/_2$ tbsps
plain flour	185 g	375 g	560 g	750 g	925 g	1.125 kg
mixed spice	$^1/_2$ tsp	1 tsp	1 $^1/_2$ tsps	2 tsps	2$^1/_2$ tsps	3 tsps
cinnamon	$^1/_2$ tsp	1 tsp	1 $^1/_2$ tsps	2 tsps	2$^1/_2$ tsps	3 tsps
PAN SIZE						
deep round (diameter)	175 mm	225 mm	275 mm	300 mm	325 mm	350 mm
deep square	150 mm	200 mm	250 mm	275 mm	300 mm	325 mm
BAKING TIMES at 150°C (in hours)						
	3-3$^1/_2$	3$^1/_2$-4	4- 4$^1/_2$	4$^1/_2$-5	5$^1/_2$-6	7-7$^1/_2$

See instructions for making the Heart Shaped Frame, opposite

HEART OF HEARTS CAKE

The secret of making this pretty shaped cake is in the cake pan. Bell shaped pans are available in three sizes from specialty cake decorating suppliers. For our cake, we used the largest pan, which holds a 500 g (1 lb) fruit cake.

Serves 25

- [ ] **550 g sultanas**
- [ ] **375 g currants**
- [ ] **375 g chopped raisins**
- [ ] **80 g mixed peel**
- [ ] **135 g glace cherries, halved**
- [ ] **60 g chopped glace fruit**
- [ ] **1 carrot, grated**
- [ ] **375 g butter**
- [ ] **1^1/$_2$ cups (255 g) brown sugar**
- [ ] **^{3}/$_4$ cup (190 mL) brandy**
- [ ] **^{3}/$_4$ cup (190 mL) fresh orange juice**
- [ ] **7 eggs, beaten**
- [ ] **1^1/$_2$ tablespoons golden syrup**
- [ ] **1 tablespoon grated orange rind**
- [ ] **2^1/$_2$ cups (375 g) plain flour, sifted**
- [ ] **^{1}/$_2$ cup (125 g) self-raising flour, sifted**
- [ ] **1 teaspoon bicarbonate of soda**

1   Place sultanas, currants, raisins, mixed peel, cherries, glace fruit, carrot, butter, sugar, brandy and orange juice in a large saucepan. Cook over medium heat, without boiling, stirring constantly until sugar dissolves.

2   Bring mixture to the boil, then reduce heat and simmer for 10 minutes. Transfer to a large bowl and allow to cool to room temperature.

3   Stir in eggs, golden syrup and orange rind. Combine plain and self-raising flours with bicarbonate of soda and fold through fruit mixture.

4   Spoon cake mixture into a greased and lined bell shaped cake pan. Bake at 150°C for 2-2^1/$_2$ hours or until cooked through. Cover cake with aluminium foil and cool in pan.

MERINGUE FROSTING

- ☐ ¹/₂ cup (125 mL) water
- ☐ 1¹/₄ cups (310 g) sugar
- ☐ 3 egg whites
- ☐ caramel food colouring
- ☐ ¹/₂ teaspoon almond essence

1 Place water and sugar in a saucepan. Cook over medium heat, without boiling, stirring constantly until sugar dissolves. Brush any sugar from sides of pan using a pastry brush dipped in water.

2 Bring syrup to the boil and boil rapidly for 3-5 minutes, without stirring or until syrup reaches the soft ball stage (or 115°C on a sweet thermometer).

3 Beat egg whites until stiff peaks form. Continue beating while pouring in syrup in a thin stream a little at a time. Continue beating until all the syrup is used, and frosting will stand in stiff peaks.

4 Add 1-2 drops of food colouring and the almond essence. Mix well to blend. Position cake on a covered board and apply frosting over the entire cake right down to the board.

5 Decorate top of cake with fresh, dried or silk flowers. Make frame as instructed in Heart Shaped Frame (right), decorate and position over cake.

❖ HEART SHAPED FRAME ❖

1 Cut two heart shapes from particle board, allowing for connecting grooves at top. Be sure the bases of the heart shapes fit snugly around cake base and that they are level.

2 Wrap the frame with 2 cm wide satin ribbon. Secure with glue.

3 Tie 3 mm wide satin ribbon bows around frame at intervals of 8 cm.

4 Tuck dried or fresh flowers into small ribbon ties. Create a posy effect at the connecting points, allowing ribbon bows to protrude from flowers.

5 Position frame and tuck flowers around cake and frame bases.

AMERICAN STYLE WEDDING CAKE

You will need to make two quantities of this mixture for the three heart shaped cakes. One quantity will fit into the largest pan and the other is divided between the two other pans.

We have used deep cake pans measuring 18 cm, 23 cm and 28 cm. These are available from specialty cookware or cake decorating shops.

- ☐ **250 g butter**
- ☐ **2¼ cups (500 g) caster sugar**
- ☐ **2 teaspoons vanilla essence**
- ☐ **6 eggs**
- ☐ **2 cups (250 g) plain flour, sifted**
- ☐ **¾ cup (90 g) self-raising flour, sifted**
- ☐ **¾ cup (190 mL) milk**
- ☐ **3 egg whites**

1   Place butter and vanilla in a large mixing bowl and beat until fluffly. Add 2 cups of sugar a little at a time, beating well after each addition until light and creamy.

2   Beat in eggs one at a time. Combine flours and add to the creamed mixture alternately with milk.

3   Whisk egg whites with remaining sugar until soft peaks form, then fold egg whites through cake mixture.

4   Spoon cake mixture into greased and lined cake pans. Bake at 160°C for 35-40 minutes for an 18 cm cake; 1 hour for a 23 cm cake and 1½ hours for a 28 cm cake. Cakes should be golden and cooked through when tested.

5   Stand cakes in their pans for 10-15 minutes before turning out onto a wire rack to cool.

BUTTERCREAM ICING

- ☐ **250 g butter**
- ☐ **2 teaspoons vanilla essence**
- ☐ **2 teaspoons almond essence**
- ☐ **½ cup (125 mL) milk**
- ☐ **1 kg icing sugar**

1   Place butter, vanilla and almond essence in a large mixing bowl. Beat until light and fluffy. Add milk a little at a time and beat until well combined.

2   Fold in icing sugar and mix until just combined. Overmixing at this stage will create undesirable air bubbles.

3   To assemble cakes, place cakes on covered boards. Spread icing over top and sides of cakes, smoothing out with a large spatula or knife. Pipe a decorative shell border around base, sides and top edge of cakes.

4   Decorate top of cakes with fresh flowers and ribbons. Position cakes on cake stands. We used individual perspex stands varying in height. These can be purchased at any cake decorating specialty shop.

SITTING PRETTY

Weddings are all about romance and what could be more romantic than this dreamy table for the wedding cake or the bride and groom.

LACE FLOWERS

We used lace continuous curtaining to drape the table and chairs, and to make our roses. Tuck small sprigs of dried flowers amongst the roses in the table swags.

1   Cut 12 cm wide strips of lace about 30-35 cm long. Fold strips double and gather raw edges together.

2   Draw up slightly. Roll lace tightly to form centre, securing it with small stitches as you go. You can also pleat lace slightly to form flatter, wider flowers or fold top edges down for a rose petal effect.

3   Fold 7 cm lengths of doubled lace for leaves so that top folded edge comes to centre. Gather raw lower edges. Tuck in amongst flowers.

TOPIARY PLACE MARKER

- [ ] **7 cm terracotta pot**
- [ ] **1.5 cm wide cream satin ribbon for roses and covering stem**
- [ ] **cream cotton doily about 45 cm in diameter**
- [ ] **3 mm wide satin ribbon for bows and trimming**
- [ ] **8 cm foam ball**
- [ ] **scraps of tulle**
- [ ] **plaster of Paris**
- [ ] **craft glue**
- [ ] **pencil**

1   Wind ribbon around pencil for stem. Glue to secure. Press pencil into centre of ball.

2   Make ribbon roses as instructed in How To Make Ribbon Roses on page 61. You will need 80 to 100 roses to cover ball. Attach roses to ball with pins.

3   Fill pot with prepared plaster. Before plaster hardens, position end of pencil in centre of pot. You will need to support the pencil in this position until it can stand alone.

4   Wrap doily around pot as shown. Secure with narrow ribbon, tied in a bow.

5   Fill top of pot with tulle. Make several bows from narrow satin ribbon and attach below ball as shown. Rest place card against pot or inside pot, against stem.

PAINTED POT PLACE MARKERS

Wedding place markers need not be the same tired old white cards. Why not make something truly unique that will be a lasting souvenir for the family and guests.

- [ ] **small terracotta pot**
- [ ] **acrylic paints**

1   Decorate pots either by painting with acrylic paints as shown or by glueing on an attractive motif cut from paper. If using latter method, paint over pot with clear-drying craft glue to seal and protect motif.

2   Paint each guest's name onto a pot and fill with flowers.

Left: Topiary Place Marker; below: Painted Pot Place Marker

SUGARED ALMONDS

A gift of sweets is a time-honoured tradition at special celebrations especially weddings. Simply place a handful of sugared almonds into the centre of a plate-sized circle of tulle. Gather up into bundles and tie up with satin rouleau ribbon in colours to complement the table setting.

Above left: Rose Place Markers
Below: How to make bread dough roses

❖
ROSE PLACE MARKER

To make about 50 roses

☐ **eight slices white bread**
☐ **Aquadhere or other clear-drying PVA craft glue**

1   Cut crusts off bread. Crumble bread between fingers. Set aside crumbs to dry out a little. Push crumbs through a sieve until very fine.

2   Mix crumbs with sufficient glue to make a sticky mass. Knead this mixture until it becomes dough-like. This transformation will occur after some time so be patient and keep working at it!

3   To make a rose, first form a bullet shape with a tiny piece of dough. Set this aside for rose centre. Take another tiny piece of dough and flatten it into an oval shape. Stretch the oval into a petal shape as in (1).

4   Fold petal around centre piece of rose one side at a time, with centre protruding a little below petal and sides overlapping as in (2).

5   Make a slightly wider petal in same way and wrap it around centre as shown in (3). Build up shape of rose in this way, adding a slightly larger petal each time (4) and (5).

6   Stretch upper edges of last few petals to curve them outwards (6).

7   To make leaves, roll out dough into an elongated shape then flatten it out. Taper both ends. Press dough onto underside of rose leaf to impress pattern of veins. Taking care not to smudge veins, cut serrations along sides with small scissors and bend leaves into shape. Make as many roses as desired and set aside to dry.

8   Mould a ball of dough about the size of a walnut for base. Flatten underside so that it sits properly. Cut a slit into top of base, at a slight angle, using a place card or playing card. After ensuring that card sits securely at desired angle, put base aside to dry out a little.

9   Attach roses and leaves to front and sides of base with hot melt glue gun or craft glue.

10 Paint individual roses with acrylic colours or spray entire arrangement with silver or gold paint.

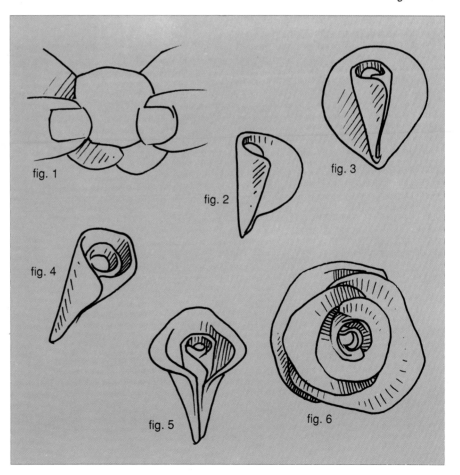

AL FRESCO LUNCH

Spread the joyous spirit by moving the lunch party into the garden where our alfresco dishes make entertaining a breeze.

SEAFOOD SALAD WITH APRICOT DRESSING

Serves 10

- [ ] 2 cooked lobsters
- [ ] 250 g cooked prawns, shelled and deveined
- [ ] 20 shelled oysters
- [ ] 3 avocados, peeled, stoned and sliced
- [ ] 1 kg nectarines, sliced
- [ ] 1 bunch watercress, washed and trimmed
- [ ] 6 shallots, chopped

APRICOT DRESSING
- [ ] $^3/_4$ cup (190 mL) apricot nectar
- [ ] 2 tablespoons white wine vinegar
- [ ] 2 tablespoons polyunsaturated oil
- [ ] 1 tablespoon brown sugar

1   Remove lobster tails from shell and slice flesh crossways. Combine lobster, prawns, oysters, avocados, nectarines, watercress and shallots in a bowl. Refrigerate until required.

2   To make dressing, combine apricot nectar, vinegar, oil and brown sugar in a screwtop jar. Shake well to combine and pour over salad just before serving.

VEAL WITH SPICY FRUIT SAUCE

Try a mixture of brandy and apple juice or just apple juice to replace the Calvados.

Serves 10

- [ ] 1.5 kg nut of veal
- [ ] 1 leek, sliced
- [ ] 1 carrot, sliced
- [ ] 1 stalk celery, sliced
- [ ] 1 cup (250 mL) chicken stock
- [ ] 1 tablespoon apple jelly
- [ ] 1 cup (150 g) currants
- [ ] 1 tablespoon Calvados (apple brandy)

SAUCE
- [ ] 2 tablespoons apple jelly
- [ ] 3 tablespoons Calvados (apple brandy)
- [ ] 2 teaspoons chopped glace ginger
- [ ] 4 tablespoons cream

1   Trim meat of all visible fat. Place leek, carrot and celery in a baking dish. Pour over stock and arrange meat over vegetables. Cover and bake at 180°C for 1 hour, basting frequently with pan liquid during cooking.

2   Remove cover and brush meat with apple jelly. Bake at 200°C for 30 minutes. Remove meat from pan and stand covered in aluminium foil. Strain cooking liquid and reserve. Discard vegetables.

3   Combine currants and Calvados in a bowl. Stand for 10-15 minutes to plump.

4   To make sauce, return reserved cooking liquid to pan. Stir in apple jelly, Calvados and ginger. Bring to the boil and cook until sauce reduces and thickens slightly. Whisk in cream and plumped currants. Cook for 1-2 minutes longer Slice meat and arrange on a serving platter. Spoon over sauce and serve.

Top left clockwise: Harlequin Salad with Strawberry Dressing; Hot Potato Salad; Cassata Cake; Sweetheart Gateau; Veal with Spicy Fruit Sauce, Snow Peas and Orange Salad; Chicken Roll with Pesto Sauce; Seafood Salad with Apricot Dressing

CHICKEN ROLL WITH PESTO SAUCE

Make this Chicken Roll the day before it is required so that it is completely chilled and will cut into neat slices.

Serves 10

- ☐ **1 large chicken, boned**
- ☐ **freshly ground black pepper**
- ☐ **30 g butter, softened**
- ☐ **1 teaspoon dried mixed herbs**

FILLING
- ☐ **3 slices wholemeal bread, crusts removed**
- ☐ **1 tablespoon sour cream**
- ☐ **2 tablespoons chopped fresh basil**
- ☐ **3 slices ham**
- ☐ **150 g canned or bottled red capsicums, drained**
- ☐ **50 g pepperoni sausage, thinly sliced**
- ☐ **6 stuffed olives, sliced**
- ☐ **4 anchovy fillets**
- ☐ **3 hard-boiled eggs**

Below: Harlequin Salad with Strawberry Dressing; opposite from top: Sweetheart Gateau; Cassata Cake

1 Lay chicken out flat on a board. Push the boned legs back into the body. Pound chicken lightly with a meat mallet to flatten. Sprinkle with pepper to taste.
2 To make filling, place bread slices over centre of chicken. Spread with sour cream and sprinkle over basil. Top bread with ham, capsicums, pepperoni, olives and anchovy fillets. Trim ends from eggs and arrange them firmly together down the centre of chicken.
3 Roll up chicken, tucking in top and bottom. Secure with string at 2.5 cm intervals. Mix butter and herbs together and rub over chicken. Bake at 180°C for 1-1¹/₂ hours or until tender and cooked through. Serve chilled, cut into slices.

PESTO SAUCE
As a timesaver, make the pesto sauce two to three days beforehand.

- ☐ **¹/₂ cup (50 g) fresh basil leaves**
- ☐ **2 cloves garlic, crushed**
- ☐ **2 tablespoons pine nuts, toasted**
- ☐ **¹/₂ cup (60 g) grated Parmesan cheese**
- ☐ **4 tablespoons olive oil**

Place basil, garlic and pine nuts in a food processor or blender and process until combined. Add cheese and oil and process until smooth.

BABY BEETS, SNOW PEAS AND ORANGE SALAD

If you blanch the snow peas and make the dressing the day before, it is just a matter of tossing all the ingredients together shortly before serving.

Serves 10

- ☐ **500 g snow peas**
- ☐ **850 g canned baby beets, drained**

ORANGE DRESSING
- ☐ **3 tablespoons polyunsaturated oil**
- ☐ **1 tablespoon tarragon vinegar**
- ☐ **1 teaspoon grated orange rind**
- ☐ **1 tablespoon orange juice**
- ☐ **1¹/₂ teaspoon sugar**

1 Boil, steam or microwave snow peas until just tender. Refresh under cold running water. Drain and pat dry on absorbent paper.

2 To make dressing, place oil, vinegar, rind, juice and sugar in a screwtop jar. Shake well to combine. Arrange baby beets and snow peas in a glass serving dish. Pour over dressing and refrigerate until required.

HOT POTATO SALAD

Prepare the dressing, cook the eggs and slice the onions, capsicum and celery the day before for ease on the day.

Serves 10

- ☐ **1 kg baby new potatoes**
- ☐ **5 hard-boiled eggs**
- ☐ **2 onions, thinly sliced**
- ☐ **1 red capsicum, seeded and diced**
- ☐ **2 stalks celery, thinly sliced**
- ☐ **2 tablespoons capers**
- ☐ **2 tablespoons chopped fresh basil**
- ☐ **freshly ground black pepper**

SOUR CREAM DRESSING
- ☐ **³/₄ cup (190 mL) sour cream**
- ☐ **3 tablespoons mayonnaise**
- ☐ **1 clove garlic, crushed**

1 Boil, steam or microwave potatoes until tender. Drain.
2 Halve eggs and combine in a bowl with potatoes, onions, capsicum, celery, capers and basil. Season with pepper.
3 To make dressing, combine sour cream, mayonnaise and garlic. Pour dressing over salad. Toss and serve.

HARLEQUIN SALAD WITH STRAWBERRY DRESSING

Serves 10

- ☐ **100 g wild rice**
- ☐ **¹/₂ cup (100 g) long grain white rice**
- ☐ **¹/₂ cup (100 g) quick cooking brown rice**
- ☐ **3 tablespoons chopped fresh mint**
- ☐ **¹/₂ cup (60 g) pumpkin seeds**
- ☐ **2 tablespoons chopped glace ginger**
- ☐ **125 g strawberries, sliced**
- ☐ **¹/₂ cup (90 g) sultanas**

STRAWBERRY DRESSING
- ☐ **125 g strawberries, hulled**
- ☐ **2 tablespoons polyunsaturated oil**
- ☐ **1 clove garlic, crushed**
- ☐ **1 teaspoon grated fresh ginger**
- ☐ **2 teaspoons honey**
- ☐ **1 teaspoon lime juice**

1 Cook wild rice in a large pan of boiling water for 20-25 minutes or until grains

burst. Add white and brown rice during last 12 minutes of cooking. Drain and set aside to cool.

2 Combine rice with mint, pumpkin seeds, glace ginger, strawberries and sultanas in a bowl.

3 To make dressing, place strawberries, oil, garlic, ginger, honey and lime juice in a food processor or blender and process until smooth. Pour dressing over salad, toss and refrigerate until well chilled.

❖

SWEETHEART GATEAU

Make the meringue layers for this special gateau up to a week in advance and store in an airtight container.

Makes 10

- ☐ **6 egg whites**
- ☐ **pinch cream of tartar**
- ☐ **1 1/2 cups (330 g) caster sugar**
- ☐ **125 g ground hazelnuts**

FILLING
- ☐ **150 g dark chocolate**
- ☐ **2 teaspoons rum**
- ☐ **300 mL thickened cream, whipped**
- ☐ **500 g raspberries**
- ☐ **icing sugar**

1 In a large mixing bowl, beat egg whites and cream of tartar until soft peaks form. Add sugar, one spoonful at a time, beating well after each addition until meringue is stiff and glossy. Fold through hazelnuts.

2 Line three oven trays with baking paper. Grease paper and dust lightly with corn-flour. Using a heart shaped cake pan as a guide, draw a 20 cm heart on each tray.

3 Spoon meringue into a large piping bag fitted with a plain tube. Pipe flat rounds within the marked hearts. Bake at 160°C for 1½ hours or until crisp and dry. Cool on trays, then transfer to wire racks.

4 To make filling, melt chocolate over hot water. Stir in rum and remove from heat. Arrange one heart on a serving plate and spread with half the chocolate mixture, half the cream and one third of the raspberries. Top with second heart and repeat with chocolate, cream and raspberries. Top with third heart and remaining raspberries. Dust lightly with icing sugar.

❖

CASSATA CAKE

Make the biscuit layer up to a week in advance and store in an airtight container. The filling can be made the day before and stored in the refrigerator.

Serves 10

BISCUIT LAYER
- ☐ **1 cup (125 g) plain flour, sifted**
- ☐ **125g unsalted butter, softened**
- ☐ **4 tablespoons chopped almonds**
- ☐ **4 tablespoons brown sugar**

FILLING
- ☐ **200 g glace fruit, chopped**
- ☐ **1 tablespoon Benedictine**
- ☐ **60 g white chocolate**
- ☐ **125 g unsalted butter**
- ☐ **3/4 cup (165 g) caster sugar**
- ☐ **2 eggs**

TOPPING
- ☐ **1 cup (250 mL) cream**
- ☐ **2 teaspoons Benedictine**
- ☐ **100 g chocolate, melted and cooled**
- ☐ **chocolate curls**
- ☐ **crystallised violets**

1 To make biscuit layer, place flour in a mixing bowl. Rub through butter with fingertips until mixture resembles fine crumbs. Add almonds and brown sugar and work into a soft paste. Press mixture into a greased and lined 28 cm x 18 cm shallow cake pan. Bake at 200°C for 20 minutes or until golden brown. Stand in pan until cool. Turn onto a wire rack.

2 To make filling, place glace fruit in a bowl and sprinkle with Benedictine. Cover and stand for 1 hour. Melt chocolate over hot water. Remove from heat and set aside to cool.

3 Beat butter in a bowl with an electric mixer until creamy. Add sugar a little at a time, beating well after each addition. Whisk in eggs one at a time. Stir in chocolate and soaked fruit. Spread mixture over biscuit layer and refrigerate for 2 hours until firm.

4 To make topping, combine cream and Benedictine in a chilled mixing bowl. Beat until thick, then fold in chocolate.

5 Using a serrated knife, halve chilled biscuit layer lengthways. Arrange one half of the biscuit side down on a serving plate and spread with half the cream mixture. Top with remaining biscuit half and decorate with remaining cream mixture, piped attractively around top edges. Sprinkle over chocolate curls and top with violets. Refrigerate until required and slice to serve.

BEAUTIFUL
BRIDE

Follow our guide to look radiant on your wedding day.

Good health and clear skin make a beautiful bride. If you take care of your diet, undertake regular exercise and follow a skin care routine which includes not only the face, but body, hands, feet and hair, you will not only look fabulous for the day, but will retain that radiance.

Many beauty therapists recommend that brides-to-be begin skin treatments at least three months before the big day. It is a good idea to visit a therapist for advice about your skin, diet and lifestyle before beginning any treatment. Facials are the best method for clearing the skin of impurities and blemishes. Even if you have good skin you should try to have a facial once a week for at least two months before the day of the wedding.

Apart from facials, a nightly bath scented with aromatic essential oils, such as lavender, for a week before the wedding is wonderfully relaxing. Chamomile has a soothing effect and is good for ensuring a sound sleep the night before the wedding, and cold chamomile teabags refresh tired eyes. Peppermint tea aids digestion and also relaxes the nervous system.

Full body massages and aromatherapy are excellent relaxation methods. Swedish massage is more active, concentrating on muscle manipulation. Fitness helps you feel good about yourself and helps you to cope with stress. Undertake any

type of exercise you enjoy: swimming, walking, aerobics, cycling or yoga. Finding a balance is the key: if you have a job where you sit for much of the day then you should try a high-energy exercise; whereas if you have an energetic job, a more relaxed exercise routine such as walking or yoga would be better for you.

Once you have your skin and body in order, it's time to consider your make up and appearance for the wedding day. Colour analysis is a good way to start, and you should think about this before you buy your gown. The

wrong white could make you look sallow or drained and exaggerate any complexion problems you may have.

Practise applying your make up, but if you don't feel confident enough to attempt it on the day, make an early booking with a beautician. Perhaps your bridesmaids, mother and mother-in-law would also like professional advice or help for the day.

The colour of the bridesmaids' outfits and bouquets must be taken into consideration when choosing make up, particularly lipstick. The safest colours are ivory white for the bride and periwinkle blue, coral pink and aqua blue for the attendants' outfits. Choose a lipstick to match the bridal party's outfits.

Manicures and pedicures (craggy heels and jagged nails can tear stockings) are the finishing touch where beauty is concerned. A manicure includes buffing the nail surface, clipping dry cuticles and moisturising the hands. Olive oil mixed with caster sugar is a good home treatment for dry hands and rough elbows. Smooth in the oil mixture with a gentle circular motion for ten minutes then remove with warm towel compresses. The mixture will remove dead cells and nourish the skin.

Nail colour is a personal preference but clear soft colours such as shell pink or pearl enamel are most popular with traditional brides. Also popular are the classic French manicures where the nail plate is given a natural pink shade and the tips are accentuated with white. For a long-lasting finish it is best to apply a base coat, then two coats of colour and a top coat. Leaving a narrow gap at either side of the nail will give the illusion of longer nails.

If you plan a honeymoon where you will be swimming, an eyelash tint may be a good idea. Usually this is done when you have a facial and will last up to six weeks. Eyebrows can be tinted too.

For women who like having smooth legs, a full or half-leg wax and bikini wax is the answer. But if you have always shaved your legs before, remember it will take at least three waxes before the legs are completely smooth because with shaving, body hair grows back at varying rates. With waxing, hair grows back at an even rate and will be much softer.

As for diet, sensible eating and drinking is the answer. You don't need to abstain completely from drinking alcohol, but cut back on social drinking and when you are dining at home. Chocolate, red wine and orange juice can exacerbate any skin problems so eat plenty of fresh fruit and steamed vegetables for a week or so before the wedding so that your skin will be clear. For clear and sparkling eyes, make sure you get plenty of sleep. Drinking water is good for you but don't go overboard! Drink enough to quench your thirst and try to have purified water as it contains less sodium than mineral water.

Start a good skin cleansing routine each morning and night if you don't already have one. Always use a specially formulated eye cleanser for the eyes. Jojoba oil or sweet almond oil is a nourishing oil for this sensitive area.

Never use soap on your face or hair. Soap strips the skin of oil rather than cleanses the skin and will leave your face dehydrated and tight, causing blackheads and spidery lines. A good cleansing milk will leave the skin feeling soft and fresh. Your finished make up will only look as good as the skin underneath. Prepare the skin well prior to make up application and remove it thoroughly afterwards and the skin will not congest or form blemishes. Make up, especially a foundation base with a total sunscreen, is excellent protection for the skin from the ravages of weather and pollution. A word of warning: if you plan a honeymoon in the sun, always wear a sunblock with a strong sun filter on the face, neck and the backs of your hands.

THE GLAMOROUS GARTER

Sweet and sexy, this garter is so simple to make and will delight any bride.

- [ ] **1 m double-edged lace**
- [ ] **1 m of 1.5 cm wide satin ribbon**
- [ ] **elastic to fit**
- [ ] **ribbon roses**

1   Join ends of lace in a flat seam to form a circle. Zigzag over seam to neaten.
2   Topstitch ribbon over centre of lace, stitching close to edges of ribbon. Cover one raw end of ribbon by overlapping other end, folding this raw end under. Leave folded end open to insert elastic.
3   Insert elastic. Secure ends.
4   Make ribbon roses as instructed on page 61 and handsew them into place.

❖ **BLUE GARTERS** ❖
The custom of throwing the bride's blue garter to the male guests dates from the fourteenth century and mirrors the throwing of the bouquet. The blue colour symbolises purity, love and faithfulness.

BOWS
FOR THE VEIL

Trim a simple veil with one of these fabulous net bows or attach one to a comb for a lovely hair accessory.

All the bows are made from strips of double layers of net, cut slightly wider than their finished width. Join the two layers together by stitching 3 mm satin ribbon down along the edges and then trimming back the net to the ribbon.

For the pink and cream bows, make around 10 loops of net, stitched into a pompom shape. Decorate with ribbon roses, glued all over, or streamers of narrow ribbon.

The cream bow shows how the ribbon that binds the sides can be stitched down the centre of double-edged lace for a different effect.

The yellow bow has a rose, made from rolled and ribbon-trimmed net, as its centre.

Photography by Alan Khan and Christopher Poulos

FLOWERS
FOR THE VEIL

For a sophisticated, but still very romantic look, trim a veil with these beautiful flowers made from silk organza.

- [ ] **sufficient silk organza for 5 small and 25 large petals**
- [ ] **fabric stiffener from a craft shop or made by mixing 1 part clear drying PVA glue with 12 parts tepid water**

1   Saturate fabric with solution. Hang up to dry, without wringing. Smooth out wrinkles as fabric dries.
2   Cut out petals.
3   Make flowers by folding stems closely around each other, beginning with smaller petals, and overlapping edges. Handsew petals into place as you go. Pull petals gently into desired shape.
4   Attach flowers to comb and veil.

❖ VEILS UNVEILED ❖

Veils were originally designed to protect the bride from evil spirits and ensure a lucky marriage. Cautious grooms insisted that the veil be thrown back after the ceremony to ensure they had the right bride!

Opposite above: a bridal veil can be held in place with real or silk flowers, a cap or, for a truly formal wedding, even a tiara; opposite below: net bows for the veil; above right top: organza flower to trim the veil; right : petal pattern for organza veil

C R O W N I N G
GLORY

*Pretty as a picture, these two beautiful bridesmaids are
wearing circlets of fresh flowers in their hair. You can make
one with fresh flowers like these or use ribbon roses to
make a colourful, long-lasting circlet.*

RIBBON ROSE CIRCLET

☐ **35 cm of 12 mm wide satin ribbon for each rose.**
☐ **35 cm of 3 mm wide satin ribbon for each bow trim.**
☐ **extra thick pipe cleaners (from craft stores)**
☐ **2 cm wide ribbon for base**

1 Twist enough pipe cleaners together to go around head. Twist a second strand of pipe cleaners around first for added strength.
2 Wind 2 cm wide ribbon around pipe cleaners, covering them completely. Glue or sew ends to secure.
3 Make ribbon roses as instructed in How To Make Ribbon Roses in desired colours and in sufficient quantity to generously cover base. Stitch or glue roses around base. Intersperse 3 mm wide bows between roses.

❖ WEDDING WAYS ❖

Some African tribes bind together the wrists of the bride and groom with braided grass.

In Czechoslovakia, rural brides wear rosemary wreaths woven for them on the eve of their wedding.

In Germany, the bride and groom hold candles trimmed with flowers and ribbons.

Greek brides carry a lump of sugar in their gloves for sweetness all her married life.

In India, the groom's brother sprinkles flower petals on the bridal couple.

❖ HOW TO MAKE RIBBON ROSES ❖

1 Roll one end of 60-90 cm ribbon about six times to form a tight tube. Sew a few stitches at base to secure (fig. A).
2 To form ribbon rose petals, fold top edge of unwound ribbon down towards you so that it is parallel to tube and folded edge is at an angle of 45° (fig. A).
3 Using basic tube as pivot, roll tube across fold, loosely at top and tightly at base (figs B and C).
4 Repeat steps 2 and 3 and continue shaping rose as you go (fig. D). Tight winding forms a bud while loose winding forms a rose.
5 Finish by turning under raw edge and stitching it to base.

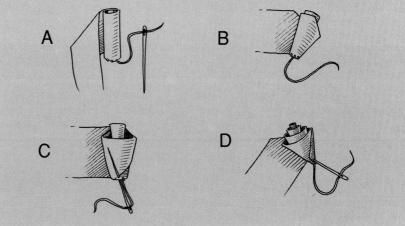

Ribbon Rose Circlet

❖
FRESH FLOWER CIRCLET

It is quite simple to make a headband or circlet from real flowers if you prefer, following the instructions on pages 68. Make a base for the flowers as instructed in Ribbon Rose Circlet, above. Remember that fresh flower circlets cannot be made too far in advance and must be handled with great care to prevent bruising the petals. A romantic circlet of rosebuds, baby carnations and gypsophila is a delightful finishing touch for a bridesmaid and well worth the little extra effort.

BRAIDED BEAUTY

You've chosen your dress and veil, and now it's time to decide on the perfect hairstyle to complement the total look. We selected this beautiful and very unusual braided style for the bride with long, straight hair. It will look best worn with a simple veil. These step-by-step pictures will serve as a guide for your hairdresser.

STEP 1
Brush hair carefully to remove all tangles before you begin. Part hair through the centre or natural parting. Form a 'V' section on one side of the part.

STEP 2
Divide the 'V' section into two. Tie ribbon to second section on back of head. Using 'figure of eight' method, wrap ribbon over and under first section and then over and under second section.

STEP 3
Repeat wrapping method, at the same time picking up extra hair on the sides of the braid and adding it to the braid. Wrap ribbon over to keep only two sections of hair in the braid. Note that hair does not cross over, only the ribbon does. Remember to pick up a new section of hair every time you wrap ribbon over.

STEP 4
Before repeating STEP 3, remove a fine strand of hair from the middle of the second section before ribbon wraps over. Use end of comb to pick up this strand.

STEP 5
Place hair strand onto first section and wrap the ribbon over it to secure. This creates loops of hair down the centre of the braid.

STEP 6
Repeat the braiding method through to the end of the hair, taking care to distribute the hair evenly around the crown. As braids pass nape, pick up from crown only.

STEP 7
Loop ribbon into a half knot to finish off.

STEP 8
Repeat for other side and tie together.

STEP 9
Lift the strands lying over centre of ribbons with a tail comb to form loops.

STEP 10
Finish off with bows and miniature roses. Cut off loose end of ribbon at the top and tuck it into the braid.

LOVE IN

If flowers are the language of love, then let them burst forth at your wedding! Flowers are a symbol of rejoicing and they can transform the plainest church or reception venue into a fantasia of colour and scent. For a lasting memory why not consider dried flower bouquets or silk flower arrangements? They save last-minute preparation, and are beautiful keepsakes. You can also preserve your fresh flowers and on page 69 we tell you how.

When choosing flowers, think in terms of your overall colour scheme, especially the colours of the bridal party's outfits and the venues. Flowers for the bridal party include bouquets or posies for the bridesmaids and flower-girls, buttonholes for the groom and his attendants and corsages for the mothers of the bride and groom. Most important, of course, is the bridal bouquet.

Think of it as an accessory – it should complement your gown and flatter your colouring and stature. Make sure it also has some sweet-smelling flowers, so that the fragrance follows you up the aisle.

A beautiful idea for informal weddings is to carry an armful of long-stemmed flowers, or, for a touch of tradition, carry a copy of your mother's or grand-mother's bouquet. A tight posy is the most suitable style for a period gown, while a trailing bouquet balances the lines of a dress with a long train.

Check with the minister before making floral arrange-ments for the church because the church may have been decorated for an earlier ceremony or pro-vide its own vases and flowers. Decorate the church with arrangements at the pulpit, the lectern and the pew ends, held

B L O O M

in place with generous satin bows, or swathe flowers as garlands along the length of the altar. Usually elaborate arrangements are best only for large, formal ceremonies.

Delicate pink and white or yellow flowers add bright splashes of festive colour. Another idea is to place a garland of flowers at the entrance of the church as a lovely frame for photographs after the ceremony.

For an informal ceremony, a garden wedding is lovely and if it is between seasons, you can heighten the impact of colour and scent by adding potted plants or shrubs. Civil marriage celebrants normally conduct garden weddings, so once you've set the date it is a good idea to book a celebrant immediately as many are booked months in advance. For garden weddings, the bride usually chooses a less

formal outfit, even a three-quarter-length dress is acceptable. Often a circlet of flowers or a wide-brimmed hat is worn in place of a train or veil. Consider what flowers will be in bloom at that time of year. Also check the sun's angle for the time of the ceremony, so that you won't be squinting or have shadows in your photographs. If your wedding is at your home or in a marquee, you can bring the garden indoors by placing lots of flowering shrubs about. Wrap garlands of flowers at either the entrance to the marquee or the house and around doorways.

Table decorations should be generous and colourful and designed to match the bridal party's colour scheme. Take care that they are not so tall as to interfere with conversation across the table.

THE LANGUAGE OF
FLOWERS

Traditionally, different flowers have been thought to carry various meanings. The ancient Greeks favoured lilies for innocence while Roman brides wore chaplets of flowers and herbs. In Germany, myrtle symbolises purity and fertility.

FLOWERS AND THEIR MEANINGS

acacia	secret love
camellia	excellence
carnation	distinction
forget-me-not	true love
daisy	innocence
gardenia	joy
honeysuckle	devotion
lily	purity
lily-of-the-valley	happiness
myrtle	purity and fertility
orange blossom	loveliness and happiness
pansy	shyness
peony	bashfulness
rose	love
rosemary	commitment and fidelity

FLORAL CALENDER

Use this seasonal guide to help you choose flowers at their best for your bouquet.

❖

SPRING
Apple blossom, azalea, blue-bell, broom, camellia, clematis, daffodil, daisy, forget-me-not, hyacinth, jasmine, lily-of-the-valley, lilac, mimosa, narcissus, polyanthus, primrose, rhododen-dron, tulip.

❖

SUMMER
Azalea, alstroemeria, aster, daisy, delphinium, fuchsia, golden rod, geranium, gladioli, hydrangea, heather, hollyhock, lupin, lily-of-the-valley, lilac, marigold, shasta daisy, phlox, peony, rhododendron, stock, sweetpea, sweet William, tiger lily.

❖

AUTUMN
Alstroemeria, amaryllis, daisy, jasmine, nerine, snowdrop.

❖

ALL YEAR ROUND
Bouvardia, carnation, chrysanthemum, freesia, gladioli, gypsophila, iris, lily, orchid, rose, stephanotis.

❖ A FAMILY HEIRLOOM ❖
Most brides want to keep their wedding gown as a lasting memento of their special day and perhaps even to pass it on to their own daughters. To store your wedding dress safely, fold it with layers of acid-free tissue paper and place it in a large box. If you want to be even more careful you can then wrap the box in a black cotton bag. Lay the box flat and store it in a cool, dry place. Many dry-cleaners will clean and package your gown for you ready for storage.

F R A G R A N T
F L O W E R S

*From formal bouquets to charming posies, flowers are the
traditional finishing touch for any wedding. Here are some
simple guidelines for making your own arrangements.*

A SIMPLE POSY

*Nothing could be more charming for a
young bridesmaid or flower girl than an
informal posy of fresh flowers. Making one
yourself is quite simple.*

1   Gather together four or more varieties
of flowers such as rosebuds, cornflowers,
gypsophila, pansies and some evergreen
foliage. Make a small bunch, using one of
each variety (A).
2   Continue adding one flower at a time,
turning the posy in your hand and wiring
the flowers to sit at an angle (A). When the
posy is complete, wind green florist's tape
around the stems, bending them slightly
as shown (B). You will need to stretch the
tape as you go for it to cling to the stems.
Decorate the finished posy with bows and
streamers of satin ribbon.

The romance of a beautiful bouquet

Photography by Alan Khan and Christopher Poulos

FLOWERS IN HER HAIR

*Flowers twined into a headband or circlet
are the perfect finishing touch for a bride or
one of her attendants. Choose flowers
that complement the bouquet and dress
and that are an appropriate size for the
wearer.*

1   To make a headband, you can either
make a covered wire base to the correct
size and wire your choice of flowers around
it or bind individually wired flowers together without a base. In both cases begin
by wiring each flower individually, covering the stems with tape then joining them
together. Start with just a couple of stems
positioned so that one side will lie flat
against the head (C). Finish both ends of
the headband in the same way with tapering blossoms pointing to the back (D).
Curve the completed headband to fit and
hold it in place with pins or ribbons (E).
2   Make the circlet in the same way as
the headband, binding the flowers onto a
prepared wire base (F) or making a circle
of wired flowers, joining the ends to complete the circle (G).

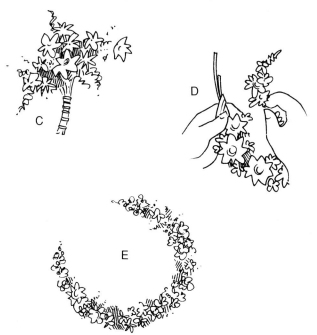

Photography by Alan Khan and Christopher Poulos

BEAUTIFUL BOUQUETS

Every bride has very special feelings for her bouquet. Wonderful blooms gathered together with ribbons and lace are a feature of any wedding party.

1   An informal bouquet, designed to be cradled or held in the hand, should be wired as little as possible. Simply lay the flowers, with the longer and stronger stems at the back. Using these as your base, build up the bouquet, tapering the top and edges. Bind the stems together carefully to secure the bouquet. To form a trail of flowers to hang from the bouquet, begin with a small flower or bud and gradually build up the shape (H). Position the trail carefully to complement the bouquet and wire it into place.

2   To form a wired, shaped bouquet, each bloom must be wired individually, covered with florist's tape and then bound together when a pleasing shape is achieved. Begin joining a few flowers together (I) by twisting the stems as shown. It may be easier to make three or four sprays which are then joined together (J). Position the largest flowers in the centre and the smaller ones at the sides, tapering to a point if desired. Bend the wires as you go so that the bouquet arches gracefully (K). Bind the stems with florist's tape and trim with lace or ribbons.

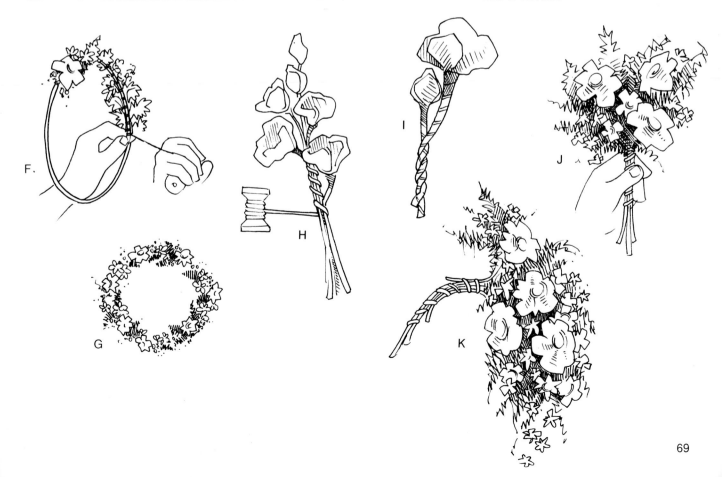

EVERLASTING MEMORIES

*When the wedding is long past, you will continue to enjoy
these reminders of your special day.*

SILK-COVERED PHOTO ALBUM

*A very special album, embroidered and
monogrammed with the bride's and
groom's initials, to hold all the memories of
their wedding day.*

- ☐ **silk taffeta to cover and two ties
  14 cm x 50 cm**
- ☐ **polyester wadding**
- ☐ **embroidery threads**
- ☐ **iron-on interfacing**

1 Measure total width of album cover
when closed plus 20 cm and length plus 2
cm. Cut out two pieces of silk this size.
Interface one cover piece.

2 Embroider front with pattern of grub
roses as shown. Instructions for em-
broidering grub roses are on page 37.

3 Place two pieces together with right
sides facing. Stitch around outside edge,
leaving opening for turning. Turn and press.
Close opening by hand.

4 Place album inside cover, matching
centres. Mark foldline for flaps. Stitch flaps
into place at upper and lower edges by
hand.

5 Place ties with right sides together and
stitch around outside edge, leaving small
opening for turning. Turn and press.
Attach to corner with small hand stitches.

This wonderful bridal wreath has been made from the dried flowers of the wedding bouquet. To preserve the flowers, spread them on a flat tray and dry them overnight in a very slow oven. They are ready to use when they feel quite papery to touch. Using a quick-drying craft glue, attach the flowers to the wreath base, adding ribbons if you wish. Attach a wire loop to the back for hanging it up.

To dry a complete bridal bouquet, without losing its shape, pour borax into a deep cake tin until a third full. Lay the bouquet on top and fill the tin completely with borax so that the bouquet is completely covered. A small paint brush is ideal for brushing borax between the petals and into tiny spaces. Cover the tin and allow it to stand for about three months. When you open the tin you will find the bouquet has been perfectly preserved.

KEEPING A
RECORD

Memories may fade but photographs are mementos which can be treasured long after the event. Plan your photographs or video to capture this once-in-a-lifetime occasion.

Choose a wedding photographer with care, one who is imaginative and reliable. Wedding photography is an art form and as such needs careful planning – don't depend on happy snaps taken by well-wishing friends and family to fill your album. If you know somebody with proven photographic skills, with good quality camera equipment, invite them to be the official photographer for the day. Alternatively, you may seek the expertise of a professional photographer.

The most important consideration when you choose a photographer is that you feel comfortable and happy with both the photographer and his or her style. Invite the photographer to your house or wherever you will be preparing for the wedding, as well as the reception venue, to see the surroundings and lighting before the event.

If you plan to have a professional photographer, begin 'shopping around' for the right person as early as possible. Visit several companies, ask to see sample wedding albums and compare the quality of work. Spend some time with the photographer before the wedding and discuss the mood you wish to capture in your photographs. If you like, ask for candid shots for your album.

Remember the happiest day of your life

Compile a list of the photographs you want and obtain quotes, this way you can compare prices. Posing for photographs can create some embarrassment, but a good photographer will take charge so as to ensure the session goes smoothly. Playing soft music can help the bridal couple relax.

Traditionally, photographs are taken at the bride's house before she leaves for the church, in front of the church before she enters with her father, in the vestry for the signing of the register and when the wedding

party emerges from the church. After the ceremony it is customary for the bridal couple, their attendants and immediate family to gather for group photographs.

Important photographs at the reception are: the bridal party seated at their table, the cake, the bride and groom, the bride and her father dancing, the groom and his mother dancing, the musicians, the bride and groom cutting the cake, the bride throwing the bouquet, the newlyweds leaving the reception and guests waving good-bye.

The ultimate record of a wedding is the video where you can experience the whole event again. When making a video, indirect soft lighting is better than direct light and causes much less discomfort for all. Avoid the common practice of a direct and powerful light attached to the camera. A high-level light source is better than eye-level.

If you plan to use a professional video film maker, ask for recommendations from your rector or reception venue and ask to see a demonstration tape. Book well in advance and make a checklist of the aspects of the ceremony and reception you wish to be filmed.

Introduce the video film maker to your master of ceremonies so he or she is aware of the program for speeches, toasts and the cutting of the cake.

Photography by Alan Khan and Christopher Poulos

SIMPLE
CELEBRATION

Imagination, in large quantities, is the most essential ingredient when preparing food for a wedding party. This menu, which serves 25, is a celebration for the tastebuds.

MINIATURE OPEN SANDWICHES

These miniature open sandwiches make wonderful finger food. To add interest and variety, use different types of bread such as rye and pumpernickel and try flavouring butters with spices and herbs, and different varieties of lettuce.

Makes 20 sandwiches.

☐ **large French breadstick**
☐ **butter or margarine**

1   Prepare all toppings (see Tasty Toppings, below) and store, covered, in the refrigerator.
2   Thinly spread butter or margarine on bread then cover with plastic food wrap until ready to use. Top open sandwiches as needed.

❖ TASTY TOPPINGS ❖
☐ cucumber slices with sour cream and caviar
☐ lettuce with smoked chicken, cherry tomatoes and coriander
☐ smoked salmon with camembert slices, avocado and lemon
☐ lettuce with Stilton and asparagus
☐ lettuce with sliced hard-boiled eggs and tomatoes
☐ rare roast beef with horseradish and watercress sprigs
☐ asparagus with mayonnaise and chopped hard-boiled egg
☐ lettuce with sour cream, oysters and chives
☐ butter lettuce with king prawns and herbed mayonnaise

COCKTAIL CHICKEN STICKS

These tasty cocktail chicken sticks are prepared and left to marinate overnight.

Serves 25

☐ **750 g chicken fillets**
☐ **good quality toothpicks, soaked in water**

MARINADE
☐ **$^3/_4$ cup (190 mL) hoisin sauce**
☐ **3 tablespoons teriyaki sauce**
☐ **4 tablespoons pineapple juice**
☐ **2 tablespoons polyunsaturated oil**
☐ **2 teaspoons grated fresh ginger**

1   Cut chicken into 2.5 cm pieces.
2   To make marinade, combine hoisin, teriyaki, pineapple juice, oil and ginger in a bowl. Add chicken and toss to coat. Cover and refrigerate for 2-4 hours or overnight.
3   Thread two pieces of chicken onto each toothpick. Grill for 4-5 minutes or until just cooked. Baste with marinade frequently during cooking.

❖ GREAT GARNISHES ❖
Food must appeal to they eye as well as to the appetite. Decorate your platters with colourful and imaginative use of garnishes such as sprigs of fresh herbs, fanned strawberries or gherkins, cherry tomatoes, capsicum rings, or even with fresh flowers.

ASPARAGUS WITH PROSCIUTTO HAM

Blanch the asparagus the day before and wrap with ham. Cover with plastic food wrap and store in the refrigerator.

Serves 25

☐ **3 bunches fresh asparagus**
☐ **9 slices prosciutto ham**

VINAIGRETTE DRESSING
☐ **4 tablespoons tarragon vinegar**
☐ **3 teaspoons wholegrain mustard**
☐ **freshly ground black pepper**
☐ **$^1/_2$ cup (125 mL) olive oil**

1   Boil, steam or microwave asparagus until just tender. Refresh under cold running water and drain.
2   Cut prosciutto into three strips lengthways. Wrap a strip of prosciutto around each asparagus spear.
3   To make dressing, combine vinegar, mustard, pepper and oil in a screwtop jar. Shake well to combine. Arrange asparagus on a serving platter and pour over dressing.

MINI QUICHES

Our delicate but filling recipes look inviting and attractive but are just a mouthful – they're perfect for eating and socialising at the same time! For easier preparation, they can be made the day before if you wish.

Makes 24

PASTRY CASES
☐ **10 sheets prepared puff pastry**
☐ **patty cake pans**

1   Cut pastry into rounds using a 6 cm cutter. Place rounds into lightly greased shallow patty cake pans. Fill pastry cases with desired filling (see Fabulous Fillings, below).
2   Bake at 180°C for 15-20 minutes or until pastry is golden brown.

SMOKED SALMON AND CRAB ROLLS

Serves 20

☐ **220g canned crabmeat, drained**
☐ **125 g ricotta cheese**
☐ **2 tablespoons capers, chopped**
☐ **2 tablespoons mayonnaise**
☐ **2 teaspoons lemon juice**
☐ **freshly ground black pepper**
☐ **few drops Tabasco**
☐ **200 g sliced smoked salmon**
☐ **1 bunch fresh dill, finely chopped**
☐ **lemon slices to garnish**

1   Combine crabmeat, ricotta, capers, mayonnaise, lemon juice, pepper and Tabasco in a bowl.
2   Spread crab mixture onto salmon slices. Roll up and cut into 2.5 cm lengths. Secure each roll with a toothpick.
3   Brush ends of each roll with water and dip into chopped dill. Garnish.

TROPICAL PRAWNS

Serves 24

☐ **24 large uncooked prawns, deveined with tails intact**
☐ **4 tablespoons cornflour**
☐ **1 cup (250 mL) mango puree**
☐ **1 cup (125 g) chopped hazelnuts**
☐ **³/4 cup (65 g) shredded coconut**
☐ **¹/2 teaspoon ground nutmeg**
☐ **2 teaspoons grated orange rind**
☐ **oil for cooking**

1   With a sharp knife, cut deeply along back of prawns, without cutting right through. Coat with cornflour, then dip in mango puree.
2   Combine nuts, coconut, nutmeg and orange rind. Press coated prawns into nut mixture.
3   Heat oil in a frypan and cook prawns for 1-2 minutes or until just pink.

❖ FABULOUS FILLINGS ❖

CARROT AND FETA FILLING
☐ **4 rashers bacon, finely chopped**
☐ **4 shallots, finely chopped**
☐ **2 carrots, grated**
☐ **125 g feta cheese, crumbled**
☐ **3 eggs**
☐ **1 cup (250 mL) milk**
☐ **1 cup (125 g) tasty cheese**

1   Place bacon and shallots in a frypan. Cook for 4-5 minutes or until bacon is crisp. Stir in carrots and cook for 2-3 minutes. Remove from heat and set aside to cool.
2   Combine feta cheese, eggs, milk and tasty cheese. Stir in carrot mixture and spoon into pastry cases.

BROCCOLI AND LEMON FILLING
☐ **1 small head broccoli, broken into florets**
☐ **3 shallots, finely chopped**
☐ **1¹/2 teaspoons grated lemon rind**
☐ **2 teaspoons wholegrain mustard**
☐ **3 eggs**
☐ **1 cup (250 mL) milk**
☐ **1 cup (125 g) grated tasty cheese**

1   Boil, steam or microwave broccoli until just tender. Refresh under cold running water. Drain and pat dry with absorbent paper.
2   Chop broccoli finely and combine with shallots, lemon rind, mustard, eggs, milk and cheese. Spoon into pastry cases.

FRENCH ONION FILLING
☐ **30 g butter**
☐ **6 medium onions, finely chopped**
☐ **3 eggs**
☐ **1 teaspoon ground nutmeg**
☐ **250 g unflavoured yoghurt**
☐ **30 g blue cheese, crumbled**
☐ **¹/2 cup (60 g) grated tasty cheese**

1   Melt butter in a frypan and cook onions for 4-5 minutes or until golden brown. Remove pan from heat.
2   Combine eggs, nutmeg, yoghurt, blue and tasty cheeses in a bowl. Stir in onion and spoon into pastry cases.

SUGAR AND SPICE

❖ **FOOD WITH FLAIR** ❖

Cake plates and boards can be covered with net, lace or pretty floral print fabrics. Tiny satin bows can peep out of the croquembouche while a lovely soft satin or taffeta bow is the perfect finishing touch for a special cake. Fresh or dried flowers, garlands of coloured ribbons or tiny 'silver' charms all add that individual touch.

CROQUEMBOUCHE

Serves 25

PROFITEROLES
- [ ] **2 cups (500 mL) water**
- [ ] **150 g butter, cut into small pieces**
- [ ] **1^1/$_2$ cups (185 g) plain flour**
- [ ] **8 eggs**

FILLING
- [ ] **300 mL thickened cream**
- [ ] **3 tablespoons icing sugar**

CARAMEL SAUCE
- [ ] **3 cups (750 g) sugar**
- [ ] **1^1/$_2$ cups (375 mL) water**

DECORATION
- [ ] **1 croquembouche cone**
- [ ] **sugared almonds**
- [ ] **small ribbon bows**

1   To make profiteroles, place water and butter in a saucepan, cover and bring to the boil over medium heat. Remove pan from heat. Uncover. Add flour all at once.

2   Beat mixture well, return to heat and stir until mixture is smooth and leaves the sides of the pan. Remove from heat and set aside to cool slightly.

3   Add the eggs one at a time, beating well after each addition until light and glossy. Place heaped teaspoonfuls of mixture onto greased oven trays. Bake at 250°C for 10 minutes, reduce temperature to 180°C and bake for 15-20 minutes longer or until puffs are golden and crisp.

4   Remove from oven and make small slits in sides of puffs to allow steam to escape. Return to oven for a few minutes to dry out. Cool completely.

5   To make filling, place cream and icing sugar in a large mixing bowl and beat until thick. Make a small hole in the base of each puff and using a piping bag fitted with a small plain nozzle, fill with a small amount of cream mixture.

6   To make caramel sauce, place sugar and water in a heavy-based saucepan and cook over medium heat without boiling, stirring constantly until sugar dissolves. Bring to the boil and boil rapidly until mixture turns golden brown.

7   Place a croquembouche cone on a serving plate. Dip the base of each puff in caramel sauce and arrange in layers around the cone. Place sugared almonds between puffs, drizzle over remaining caramel sauce and finally decorate with small ribbon bows. Stand at room temperature in a cool place until required, no longer than six hours.

❖ COOK'S TIP ❖

Croquembouche cones are available at specialty kitchen shops or from commercial kitchenware suppliers. If you find it difficult to buy a cone, you can easily make one by forming thick cardboard into a cylindrical shape and covering it with aluminium foil.

MEXICAN WEDDING BISCUITS

This is an adaptation of the original Mexican wedding cookie recipe. The biscuits can be made up in advance and stored in airtight containers. Dust with extra icing sugar before serving.

Serves 25

- [ ] **250 g butter**
- [ ] **1 teaspoon almond essence**
- [ ] **$^1/_2$ cup (90 g) icing sugar, sifted**
- [ ] **$^1/_2$ cup (60 g) chopped almonds**
- [ ] **2 cups (250 g) plain flour, sifted**
- [ ] **icing sugar**

1   Place butter, almond essence and icing sugar in a large mixing bowl. Beat until creamy. Stir in almonds, then fold in flour. Refrigerate for 30 minutes.
2   Roll mixture into small balls about 2.5 cm in diameter. Place on greased oven trays and refrigerate for 30 minutes. Bake at 180°C for 20 minutes.
3   Remove biscuits from trays and roll in icing sugar while still warm. Set aside to cool, then store in airtight containers until required.

LOVE CAKE

Serves 25

- [ ] **7 egg yolks**
- [ ] **2$^1/_4$ cups (500 g) caster sugar**
- [ ] **1$^1/_2$ cups (230 g) semolina**
- [ ] **2 cups (320 g) ground almonds**
- [ ] **2 tablespoons rosewater**
- [ ] **2 tablespoons liquid glucose**
- [ ] **$^1/_2$ teaspoon grated lemon rind**
- [ ] **$^1/_2$ teaspoon ground nutmeg**
- [ ] **$^1/_2$ teaspoon ground cardamom**
- [ ] **$^1/_2$ teaspoon almond essence**
- [ ] **8 egg whites**

1   Place egg yolks in a large bowl and beat until light and fluffy. Add half the sugar a little at a time, beating well after each addition, until creamy.
2   Stir in semolina, almonds, rosewater, glucose, lemon rind, nutmeg, cardamom and almond essence.
3   Beat egg whites with remaining sugar until glossy. Fold in almond mixture and spoon into a greased, lined 20 cm deep round cake pan. Bake at 150°C for 1$^1/_2$ hours or until golden and firm to touch.

❖ DECORATING THE CAKE ❖

Gather a length of doubled organza into a ruffle for the cake to sit on, then pin a strip around outside. Pin a bow into place. Place a doily onto cake and dust with icing sugar. Remove doily before serving.

PISTACHIO AND STILTON GRAPES

To serve these delicious morsels you might like to do as we have done and arrange them in the shape of a bunch of grapes. If you have either a real or ornamental grape vine, use some of the leaves to decorate the plate.

Makes 30

- [ ] **125 g cream cheese, softened**
- [ ] **60 g Stilton cheese, crumbled**
- [ ] **2 tablespoons light sour cream**
- [ ] **30 large seedless green grapes**
- [ ] **125 g finely chopped pistachio nuts**

1   Beat cream cheese, Stilton and sour cream in a small bowl until smooth.
2   Coat grapes with cheese mixture and roll in pistachio nuts to coat. Refrigerate until firm.

❖ CUTTING THE CAKE ❖

The bride and groom traditionally cut the first slice of wedding cake together using a silver knife, to ensure that they will have children.

Opposite: Wedding sweets including Croquembouche, Mexican Wedding Biscuits, Love Cake. Right: Pistachio and Stilton Grapes

THROWING THE
BOUQUET

You've thrown the bouquet and bid farewell to your guests, and now begins a new life with your companion. After months of planning and weeks of parties, opening presents, organising your new home and celebrating your marriage with friends and relatives, the honeymoon is just for you. It's the opportunity for romance, relaxation, adventure maybe, but most importantly for getting to know each other, this time as husband and wife, before returning to the routine of everyday life.

Keeping in mind that you may be a little tired after the wedding, it can be a good idea to spend your wedding night at a local motel or hotel and leave at your leisure the following day for your well-deserved holiday.

Beachcombing on a tropical island may be your idea of an idyllic holiday. For others it may be backpacking through a national reserve. Whatever your choice, make plans and bookings well in advance of your wedding. And remember to include all these costs, such as passport fees, vaccinations, transport, tips and souvenirs, in your initial budget.

Current passports can be amended to include your married name if you wish. If you do not hold a passport and you need one for your honeymoon, you will have to meet all the appropriate legal requirements that apply where you live, so give

A new life together

Photography by Alan Khan and Christopher Poulos

yourself plenty of time to deal with the paperwork.

Unforeseen things can upset the best-laid plans, so it is advisable also to take out travel insurance. The four basic things you should insure against are: loss of money paid in advance for travel, tickets and accommodation; loss of baggage; extra expenses if you are delayed because of strikes or a disaster and have to make alternative arrangements and medical expenses.

If you are going abroad it is a good idea to take most of your money in the form of travellers' cheques plus a small amount in local currency for taxis, porters

and hotels. Be sure to take a careful note of cheques and numbers in case of theft or loss.

Give careful consideration to your wardrobe – pack clothes which can mix-and-match. Take one pair of sensible walking shoes or sandals and a pair of court shoes for more formal attire. For most destinations, a jacket, jeans, skirt, shorts and T-shirt, a couple of blouses, swimsuit and one or two uncrushable dresses should be plenty. For men, sports clothes, shorts and T-shirts, a sweater, and bathers are fine. It is a good idea to pack a tie also because dress regulations could otherwise exclude you from being able to dine or dance at certain venues.

While sorting out what clothes to take on your honeymoon, it is the ideal opportunity to consider your entire trousseau and your wardrobe for the first year of marriage. It should include lingerie, clothing for each season, accessories, luggage and household items such as bed linen, bath towels and cookware. Much of the latter will probably come from presents and shower teas.

Lingerie should include a negligee and gown, summer and winter nightgowns, sets of slips, bras and knickers, hosiery, and winter and summer dressing gowns.

The best advice is always to buy quality goods and, when choosing clothes, to pick colours which will co-ordinate well.

COOKING GLOSSARY

TERM	MEANING
Baste	To moisten meat or vegetables with raw juices during cooking
Beetroot	Regular round beet
Bicarbonate of soda	Baking soda
Breadcrumbs, fresh	1 or 2 day old bread made into crumbs
Breadcrumbs, packaged	Use a commercial package of crumbs
Butter lettuce	Round lettuce
Capsicum	Sweet pepper
Cheese, tasty	A firm good-tasting cheddar cheese
Colbassi sausage	A type of salami with paprika
Cornflour	Cornstarch, substitute arrowroot
Cream	Light pouring cream
Essence	Extract
Ginger	Fresh ginger, ginger root. Preserved ginger is root ginger cooked in syrup
Golden syrup	Substitute honey
Hoisin sauce	Chinese barbecue sauce
Liquid glucose	Glucose syrup, available from decorating suppliers
Mango puree	If unavailable, puree canned mango slices
Mignonette lettuce	Little gem lettuce
Mustard, wholegrain	A French style of textured mustard with crushed mustard seeds
Nut of veal	A cut of veal from the top of the leg
Polyunsaturated oil	Vegetable oil high in polyunsaturated fats such as corn, soya or sunflower oil
Prepared puff pastry	Ready-rolled puff pastry. If unavailable, use thawed frozen puff pastry, thinly rolled
Shallots	Spring onions
Snow peas	Mangetout peas
Sour cream	Commercially soured cream.
Stock	Homemade gives best result, but for convenience substitute 1 stock cube for every 2 cups water
Thickened cream	Whipping cream
Tomato paste	Tomato puree

THANK YOU NOTES

We would like to thank the following generous individuals and companies who assisted in the preparation of this book: The Australia East India Company for supplying the beautiful glasses; Australian Squatters Company of Willoughby, New South Wales for supplying garden accessories; Sharon Blain for the very clever hair styling; Canning Vale Spinning Mills, Sydney for supplying our lovely cotton towels; Stephen Clarke for creating the American Style Wedding Cake; Cottage and Lace for the hand-painted pots and sunhat; the Fish Marketing Authority for providing the prawns and lobster; Home Yardage, New South Wales for the plain fabrics; Liberty for supplying all our pretty printed fabrics; Lifestyle Imports and Limoges for the beautiful china; Leo Lynch and Sons of Flemington Markets, New South Wales for the lovely flowers; McCalls Patterns for their Heritage Trims; Myer Australia for the Vogue pattern wedding dress no. 1519; N.Z. Berries for providing the berries; Offray for the wonderful ribbons; Pat Ray for creating the Traditional Wedding Cake; Royal Atlantic Salmon for supplying the smoked salmon; Julia Stewart of Lindfield for her expert assistance with make up and beauty advice; Sydney Rock Oysters for supplying the oysters; R. P. Symonds for the beautiful crystal and silverware; Village Pharmacy, Lindfield, New South Wales for lending bathroom accessories; Wendy B's florists of Mosman, New South Wales for the wedding bouquet.

We would also like to thanks Admiral Appliances; Black & Decker (Australasia) Pty Ltd; Blanco Appliances; Knebel Kitchens; Leigh Mardon Pty Ltd; Master Foods of Australia; Meadow Lea Foods; Namco Cookware; Sunbeam Corporation Ltd; Tycraft Pty Ltd, distributors of Braun Australia and White Wings Foods.

INDEX

FOOD INDEX